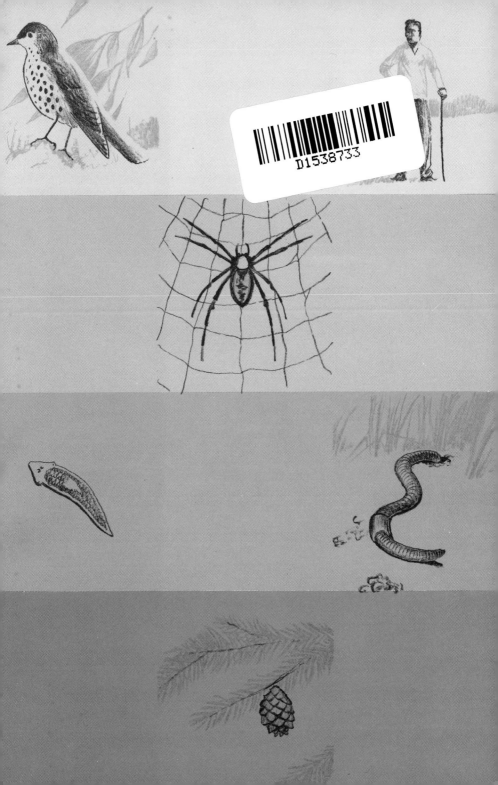

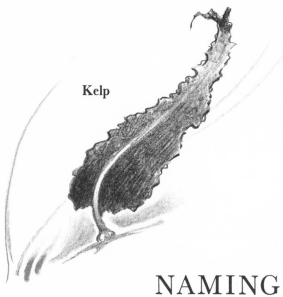

Kelp

NAMING
LIVING
THINGS

The Grouping of Plants and Animals

NAMING
LIVING
THINGS

The Grouping of Plants and Animals

By Sarah R. Riedman

Illustrated by Jerome P. Connolly

On the coldest day in 2 years (2-5-67) -13°
I brought in The original illustrations for
This book - Jerome P. Connolly

RAND McNALLY & COMPANY

CHICAGO   NEW YORK   SAN FRANCISCO

The author wishes to thank Mr. Gerald V. Zelenka, teacher of biology, Clifton, New Jersey High School, for reading the manuscript and for checking the pictures, and Mr. Jerome P. Connolly, the artist, for his careful work. Mr. Zelenka's generous help and suggestions, and Mr. Connolly's beautiful, accurate pictures have made this a better book.

Trillium

CONTENTS

CHAPTER   PAGE

A Note to the Reader *9*

1   Grouping and Naming *11*

2   The Two-Name System *18*

3   Two Kingdoms *29*

4   The World of Plants *36*

5   Backbone or Not? *52*

6   Top Rung of the Soft-Bodied *65*

7   Enter the Backbone *82*

8   The First on Land *92*

9   Equipped for Flight *102*

10   What's New About Mammals? . . .   *112*

11   Here *You* Are *122*

     Index *125*

ILLUSTRATIONS

Kelp 1
Finding a book in the library 2
Trillium 4
Fishbowl 11
Aristotle's "ladder of nature" 13
Spurge 14
Skeleton of a bird and a man 15
Grass, lily, and orchid, with embryo 17
Cap stuffed with flowers 18
Seed-eating, flesh-eating, and water bird 21
Flower, with reproductive parts 22
Linnaeus, equipped for expedition 23
Tulip and daisy 25
Red and rabbit-foot clover 26
Microscope 29
Typhoid bacillus, trypanosome, vorticella,
    and Euglena 30
Honey bee on wild strawberry 31
Photosynthesis 33
Mushrooms 35
Red algae 36
Diatoms in water 37
Plankton in the ocean 38
Mushroom and toadstool; Lichen 40
Peat moss in a bog 42

Ferns 43
Horsetails; Club mosses 44
Pollen tube; Oak and pine leaves with seeds . . . 45
Male and female white pine cones 46
Venus flytrap plant 47
Fertilization process 48
Angiosperms: Buttercup, lily, iris 49
More Angiosperms 50
Brown bat 52
Ameba; Paramecium 54
Stentor 55
Sponge 56
Hydra 57
Planaria; Tapeworm 59
Ascaris, hookworm, and trichina 60
Earthworm, sandworm, and leech 62
Starfish 63
Sea-urchin, sand-dollar, sea-cucumber, and
    sea-lilies 64
Slug; Snail 66
Oyster, clam, scallop, and mussels 67
Squid 68
Crayfish molting 69
Lobster, showing body plan 71
Daphnia, sow bug, and hermit crab 72
Millipede and centipede 73
Trapdoor spider, scorpion, tick,
    horseshoe crab, and mite 74
Deer fly, cucumber beetle, and grasshopper 75
Metamorphosis of Monarch butterfly 76
Water boatman, back-swimmer, and squash bug . . . 77
Termites, tunneling into wood 78
Beehive, with queen, drone, worker, egg,
    and larvae 79
Cicada and aphids 80
Molluscs 81
Sea lamprey 82
Sunfish, showing fins 84
Crappie and perch 85

Silverfish; Sea horse 86
Tiger shark; Mackerel 87
Angel fish laying eggs around water plants 88
Frog, tadpole, and eggs 89
Tadpole heart and frog heart 90
Green sea turtle 92
Pilot black snake 94
Copperhead snake 95
Pointed turtle 97
Crocodile 98
Alligator 99
American chameleon, salamander, and
    horned toad 101
Sparrow 102
Archaeopteryx 103
Ostrich and penguin 105
Canada goose and Downy woodpecker 106
Barn owl; Bluejay 107
Beaks of various birds 108
Albatross; Common tern 109
Ostrich and mallard duck 110
Chicken, sparrow, bat, penguin, heron,
    woodpecker, and hummingbird 111
Kangaroo; Armadillo 114
Blue whale; Beaver 116
Shrew 118
Lemur and tarsier 120
Chimpanzee 121
Primitive man, hunting 123
The human race 124

A NOTE
TO THE
READER

Before you start to read this book, there are two things you will need to know about the pictures.

First, about the color: If the artist had made all the plants and animals in their real colors, he would have had to use all the colors of the rainbow. Since this book is not intended to be used as a guide in identifying these plants and animals when you see them in their natural surroundings, that much color was unnecessary. The pictures are included to make the text easier to understand—to show you shapes, differences, and likenesses.

The pictures would have accomplished their purpose if they had been drawn in outline, in only one color. The added color is to make the book more attractive and to give special emphasis in certain places. The artist chose colors that seemed to him most pleasing.

In real life a bluejay is blue, gray, black, and white; in these pages it is shown in brown. There are books that will show you the bluejay, the other animals, and the plants in their true colors.

Second, size: It is not easy to show, in pictures, such large animals as the whale, shark, or ostrich in their proper size, nor in their comparative size when they are

9

placed next to a bat or a shrew. In some of the pictures, the artist has included background—showing trees, or other familiar things that will give you some idea of the comparative size of the plant or animal in the foreground. But most of the pictures show only special features and characteristics, which illustrate the text.

The identification books mentioned above usually tell you something about the actual size of the plant or animal pictured.

S.R.R.

1

GROUPING
AND
NAMING

Suppose you went to your library to find a special book. And suppose, when you got there, you discovered that everything had been changed around: all the large books were on one shelf, and all the small ones on another; all the green-covered books in one place, all the red in another, the blue in still another place. How would you find the one you were looking for? This kind of arrangement would be no better than having all the books in the library piled in a heap from floor to ceiling.

If you tried to list all the different kinds of living things in your back yard, in the park, the zoo, the pond, on the farm, in the forest, at the edge of the ocean, or even in your fishbowl you could easily count up to a hundred in a few minutes—if you knew the names of all of them. Maple and willow trees, robins, different kinds of grass, dandelions, squirrels, lions, frogs, amebas, muskrats, cows, pigs, ferns, snails, sandpipers, turtles, goldfish, spiders, mushrooms and, of course, cats and dogs are only some of the more-than-a-million different kinds of living things to be found in these and other places on the earth. Some of these things, like Amebas, are too tiny to see without a microscope. Some, like the whale or the giant redwood tree, are so big that you could not take them in with one glance.

And what an assortment of shapes you would find! The things that move do so in hundreds of different ways —some with feet, others with wings or fins, some crawling on their bellies, and some moving only inside a shell. How differently they breathe, what a variety of foods they eat, and how many ways they have of growing and reproducing themselves! Some see and hear, others feel or smell their way, but all are alive.

Straightening out the books in the library would be a much easier job than unscrambling all these creatures and plants and sorting them into groups. And after they were sorted how would you decide what names to give them?

These were the problems faced by the earliest men of science. First they had to arrange the plants and animals in groups—or classes and families. How to name every type of living thing was another job to be tackled later.

A GREEK PHILOSOPHER BUILDS A LADDER OF LIFE

Almost 2,500 years ago, Aristotle, a Greek, and one of the greatest philosophers of all time, decided to compare and classify the many plants and animals he had collected. He called his scheme the "ladder of nature." He said: "Nature proceeds little by little from things lifeless to animal life." He decided that plants came next on the ladder after lifeless things. And then, different kinds of animals moved up the ladder, with man at the very top.

MAN

CAT

DUCK

ALLIGATOR

FROG

FISH

INSECT (Grasshopper)

SNAIL

STARFISH

SPONGE

AMEBA
        PARAMECIUM

ANGIOSPERM (Flowering plant)
        GYMNOSPERM (Pine)

FERN   MOSSES

Aristotle's "Ladder of Nature"

Spurge

Following this idea, Aristotle arranged his collection from the bottom up, starting with the simplest and going on to the most complicated. In his ladder of life he divided all animals into two groups. Today we call them "vertebrates"—animals with a backbone—and "invertebrates" —soft-bodied animals or those without a backbone, but Aristotle, of course, gave them Greek names. The first group, he said, contains all those that have red blood, and either hatch their young from eggs, or bring them forth alive. In the second group are animals without red blood, that reproduce mostly by growing buds.

Aristotle made separate groups for fishes; for egg-laying, four-footed animals; for birds; for four-footed animals that bring forth their young alive; for the cetaceans that include the whale and dolphin; and finally for man.

These groups are still used today, even though Aristotle's classification was incomplete, and in many ways incorrect. Certainly he can be credited with beginning the system that would bring order out of chaos.

For many centuries little was added to Aristotle's system of arranging living things in orderly compartments. Beginning with the sixteenth century, naturalists in central Europe began to describe plants and animals, making faithful drawings of what they saw. The drawing of spurge, a medicinal plant, is like those they made. The same man tried to show how the skeleton of a man resembled that of a bird. The lines in the picture point to similar parts in the two. The resemblance is especially plain in the limbs.

Most of these sixteenth-century naturalists were good observers, but they were handicapped because they had

The skeleton of a bird, and of a man, showing resemblances

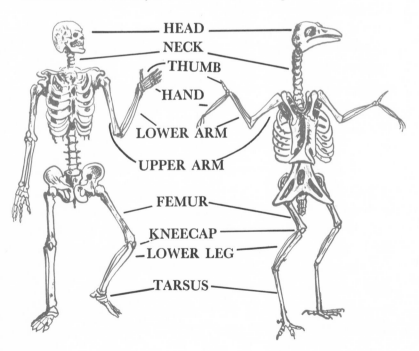

no names for individual animals. So, when they wanted to write about them, they had to use long descriptions, like this one by Thomas Moufet. This is part of his story about grasshoppers and locusts:

> "Some are green, some black, some blue. Some fly with one pair of wings, others with more; those that cannot either fly or leap, they walk; some have longer shanks, some shorter. Some there are that sing, others are silent. And as there are many kinds of them in nature, so their names were almost infinite. . . ."

It is as if you had no first and last name. If a friend wanted to talk to another friend about you he would have to say something like this: "He's (she's) a boy (a girl) five feet tall, weighs 100 pounds, has straight black hair, brown eyes, a short nose, large ears, and a thin, squeaky voice!" That's the way it was with plants and animals. The detailed description only made it harder to sort them out into groups. A system was sorely needed to clear a path in this jungle of fanciful descriptions.

LEAVES OF A KIND

Matthias de l'Obel was a Flemish botanist who came to England as a young man. He dedicated his first book (1570) to Queen Elizabeth I. Later he was botanist to King James I. The plant Lobelia is named after him.

He tried to put into one class all the plants having leaves that seemed to him to be similar. He started with grasses, lilies, and orchids which have simple (one-blade), long, narrow, pointed leaves with parallel veins. It is now known that these do belong to one large class of plants. But it is not the shape of their leaves that makes this so. It is the fact that the budding plant, or embryo, has only one seed leaf.

Following out this idea that the leaf shape determines the type, l'Obel put into a large assorted group such different plants as hickory, hemlock, and ferns. The fronds of the fern, the needles of the hemlock, and the leaflets of the compound hickory leaf, he thought, resembled each other. Actually, these three plants belong to widely separated groups. Besides, in this scheme there was no room for such plants as the mosses whose leaves are arranged in a spiral.

Many other botanists struggled for nearly two more centuries with the problem of naming and grouping.

Grass, lily, and orchid, showing an embryo and a seed leaf

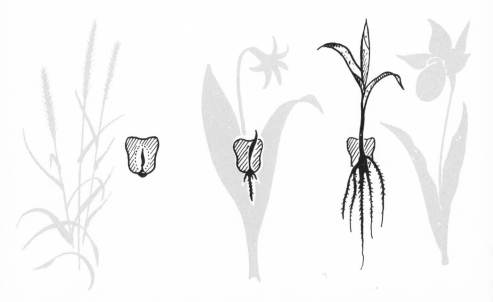

2

THE
TWO-NAME
SYSTEM

Carl von Linné was born in 1707 in Rashault, Sweden, a town no longer on the map. His father, a village pastor, cultivated a flower garden where Carl first learned to love flowers and to remember their common names. He had his own small garden, and realized quite early that there must be flowers in the rest of the world, perhaps very different kinds.

His mother was distressed over his childish habit of stuffing his trouser pockets and cap with flowers. She scolded, but to no avail, especially since her husband encouraged the boy to study "God's earthly creations." On his lonely walks in the woods he stroked their pretty petals and shiny leaves, and carried his finds back in his collecting box.

Carl went to school some thirty miles from home. His father wanted him to be a pastor, like himself. But Carl's teachers decided he would never be a scholar. They advised his parents not to waste any more money for the education of a boy who just couldn't get Latin through his head. They thought he should prepare for a trade such as shoemaking. (Oddly enough, it was this "dunce" who gave Latin names to the animals and plants he studied for the rest of his life. He even Latinized his name to Linnaeus, which is the way he has since been known to the world.)

It was plain that Carl would never make a minister. He might have become a cobbler, but the village doctor persuaded his parents that Carl ought to study medicine. The doctor saw great promise in the boy, and offered to take him into his own home to instruct him until he could go to the university. His parents decided not to stand in their son's way. They thought the doctor might be right about Carl's abilities.

In those days the study of plants was an important part of the study of medicine, because herbs were used as medicines just as drugs came to be used later. A French botanist, Joseph Pitton de Tournefort, was an accepted authority on plant description. He had traveled widely through Europe and the Near East and had diligently collected all the plants he could find. He wrote a guide book, in which he classified plants by the shape of the flower. Tournefort placed plants with small flowers in the same group with those that had no flowers.

The doctor, Linnaeus's sponsor and teacher, tried to get him to use Tournefort's guide, but Linnaeus found it confusing. He thought it shouldn't lump two trees together simply because both had red fruit, when they were very different in other ways. And he couldn't see why the strawberry plant and the lily of the valley were in the same group just because both had white petals. Besides, Tournefort divided plants into trees, bushes, and herbs, and Linnaeus wondered where the mosses fitted in.

Even though Tournefort's classification was not satisfactory, he did one important thing. He separated different living things into groups called genera; each type belonged to a particular genus, with its own scientific name. Aristotle had used the same term, but in Greek rather than Latin.

But single plants still had no labels and had to have long descriptions. It was hard to distinguish one from the other. A single plant often had many different names, or several different plants had the same name.

Linnaeüs was determined that some day he would clear a path through this dark jungle of names. But first he completed his studies at Lund University. Then, in 1728, with the little money his father could gather, Linnaeus went on to the great University of Upssala where he enjoyed the good library and the garden for students— especially for medical students interested in botany. He decided to learn everything he could about plants and animals from books written by the early naturalists. From the library he carried home a load of Latin books. His Latin was poor and his handwriting worse, but his ambition to make sense out of the chaotic disorder never left him. He would devise a system even if he were the only one to use it!

He examined the drawings of bird beaks and claws. How different they were! Some birds had short, thick beaks. These, Linnaeus decided, must be the seed-eaters, whose beaks were suitable for cracking seeds. Others had powerful beaks and large, curved claws. These must be the flesh-eating birds of prey who tore into the creatures they captured. Water birds had webbed toes for swimming, and bills for straining food from the mud.

Seed-eater (Towhee)

Above: Flesh-eater (Sharp-shinned hawk); Below: Water bird (Ruddy duck)

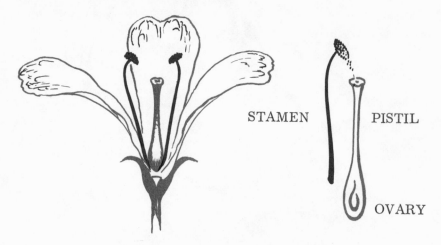

A flower and its reproductive parts

With the utmost care Linnaeus examined the reproductive, or sexual, parts of flowers. He was convinced that they must be of importance to the life of plants. In fact, he decided that this could be the basis for classifying them, and wrote a short paper about this method of classification. It impressed his teachers so much that he was made assistant to the professor of botany.

The otherwise undistinguished pupil had a passion for classification. He would classify rocks, minerals, and even diseases, in addition to plants and animals. Finally his talents as a systematic thinker were recognized by the Academy of Science at Upssala and, in 1732, he was chosen to make a one-man collecting expedition in Lapland. For the next five months Linnaeus traveled nearly 5,000 miles, exploring Lapland and much of northern Norway and Sweden.

This is the way he described his meager equipment:

"My clothes were a light coat of linsey-woolsey, leather breeches, a round wig, a green cap and a pair of half-boots. I carried a small leather bag containing one shirt, two pair of false sleeves, two vests, an inkstand, pen-case, microscope and telescope, a gauze cap to protect from gnats, a comb, my journal and a parcel of paper for drying plants, my manuscript Ornithology . . ."

We see him in this gear in the picture below.

It is said that this 5,000-mile trek cost only $125. On foot, suffering all kinds of hardship, hunger, and fatigue, Linnaeus crossed the Lapland Peninsula to the Arctic Ocean, and came back again along a parallel route. He climbed high precipices, crossed running streams, endured

extremes of heat and cold, fought off mosquitoes, observing and collecting all he could carry with him. On this solo trip, with only occasional help from two Lapps, he studied many wild animals and discovered one hundred new kinds. During his travels he began to collect for his famous *Systema Naturae (Classification of Living Things)*.

He was too poor to complete his medical studies. He now had to earn his living, so had to postpone becoming a doctor. Later, however, with the help of the girl he married, he returned to study in Holland, and obtained his degree, partly supporting himself by tutoring and lecturing.

While in Holland Linnaeus got a position as medical attendant to an Amsterdam banker, but soon he took over the directorship of his employer's botanical garden. In 1735, he published his great work, the *Systema;* in a later edition he introduced the classification for which he is famous. He took trips to Germany, France, and England on further scientific expeditions, and finally returned to Stockholm to practice medicine.

By 1742, after publishing several books on botany, his fame had spread. He was then appointed Professor of Natural History at Upssala, where his popularity as a teacher attracted crowds of students. He did not keep these young people in his lecture hall. Instead he sent them out on expeditions to many parts of the known world. The specimens they brought back to Sweden were described and classified in the edition of the *Systema Naturae* which appeared in 1758.

Linnaeus did away with long wordy descriptions of each plant and animal and substituted a name and a proper place in his classification system for each one. Thus, every living thing he knew about had a position in his system. First it was placed in a class, which was divided into several groups called orders. Each order was divided into a number of genera (Tournefort's term), and each genus separated by species.

Plant or animal individuals that are alike in their appearance, structure, and behavior and are sharply marked off from another group of individuals are called "species": a horse can be distinguished from a donkey, and a goat from a sheep, just as easily as a cat from a dog or a tulip from a daisy. Species breed only with each other and have common ancestors. Cats mate with cats and produce kittens; dogs mate with dogs and give birth to puppies. There are certain exceptions, but this is the general rule in nature. If you know the animal, you will recognize its species. You will not mistake a horse for a donkey or a zebra.

It is easy to distinguish between a tulip and a daisy

NAMING LIVING THINGS

Species naturally fall into groups of similar kinds, which are the genera. The horse, donkey, and zebra belong to the genus Equus. Red clover, white clover, and rabbit-foot clover, each a different species, belong to the genus Trifolium (three-leaved), and their names are *Trifolium pratense* (growing in meadows), *Trifolium repens* (creeping), and *Trifolium arvense* (from cultivated fields).

For both plants and animals the genera are in turn grouped into families, families into orders, orders into classes, classes into subphyla, subphyla into phyla. As new differences were found among genera, the "family" was introduced. Linnaeus had not used this classification.

Linnaeus divided animals into the following classes: Fishes, Reptiles, Birds, Mammals, Vermes, and Insects. In the last two groups he included all the classes of animals without a backbone.

His classification was deficient in many ways, and some groupings turned out to be incorrect, as naturalists dis-

Left: Red clover (Trifolium pratense); Right: Rabbit-foot clover (Trifolium arvense)

covered more and more kinds of plants and animals. His classification system has been improved, but the world does owe to Linnaeus the binomial, or two-name, system of living things.

Scientific names always have at least two words, just as people's names do—Smith, the family name and John, the given name. Just as two names identify a person more easily, they make it easier to identify a particular plant or animal. The genus is written first, with a capital letter, followed by the species, with a small letter. And Latin is the language always used for scientific names.

Let us take the familiar grass, timothy. It has a brush-like cylindrical cluster of tiny flowers. There are several kinds of timothy but, as a group, they belong to the genus called Phleum (marsh grass). *Phleum pratense* is wild timothy, often seen along roadsides or vacant city lots; *Phleum arenarium* (sandy) is a cultivated annual plant.

Or, let us see how this applies to a common animal, the cat. *Felis domestica* is the scientific name for the domestic cat. Its relatives in the same genus are *Felis tigris,* the tiger, *Felis leo,* the lion, and *Felis pardus,* the leopard. The dog belongs to a different genus. Whatever you call your dog, according to the binomial system its name is *Canis familiaris*; his close relative, the wolf, is *Canis lupus.*

Homo sapiens—that is you. *Homo sapiens* is the scientific name for man. *Homo* is the genus, and *sapiens* the species. It means man, the reasoner.

In the late 1700's something new was added to the grouping and naming of living things. The evolutionists showed that, in hundreds of millions of years, living things had gradually changed. Therefore, they could now be grouped by their structures, which had evolved as a result of the changes. For example, first there existed only spine-less animals, or animals without a backbone. In the course of many eras, some animals developed a backbone. You remember that Aristotle divided all animals into two groups—invertebrates (the soft-bodied) and vertebrates (animals with a backbone), although it was Jean Baptiste de Monet Lamarck who gave the groups these names, long after Aristotle's time.

Lamarck, a Frenchman, was born in 1744. First a botanist and a medical doctor, he later turned to the study of animals. In his time scientists and people in general held firmly to the idea that species had always existed just as they were then. Lamarck, however, believed that species changed, forming a progression—"a natural sequence." He taught that living organisms had a con-tinuity, along a scale, in which each species differed only a little from its neighbor. In this, he came fairly close to the modern theory of evolution which we owe to Charles Darwin, the English naturalist.

Darwin's expedition with the *H.M.S. Beagle* in South America in the 1830's, and his later studies in England, convinced him that every species of plant and animal constantly changes, though so slowly that the change is not noticeable from generation to generation. Darwin's idea was that when conditions of life suddenly changed, those species that were not equipped to adjust to them died out, while those survived that possessed the necessary structures for life under the new conditions. When great portions of the seas dried out, the creatures that had the beginnings of lungs could breathe air, and so could sur-vive on dry land.

3

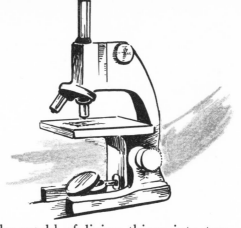

TWO
KINGDOMS

Biologists divide the world of living things into two kingdoms: plants and animals. In many ways plants and animals are different, but in almost as many ways they resemble each other. In fact, the tiniest plants and animals are so much alike that you would wonder which compartment to put them in.

On the next page are three one-celled organisms as they would look under a microscope. Two of these are one-celled animals and one is a plant. Can you tell which? All three are colorless and can move in a drop of water. The trypanosome and vorticella are Protozoa, the simplest animals. Trypanosomes cause sleeping sickness, and vorticella is a harmless creature found in pond scum. The typhoid bacillus belongs to the Bacteria. Bacteria are microscopic plants.

And on the next page, also, is one that seems to lead a double life. It is called Euglena. At one end of its spindle-like body it bears a long whip-like thread called a flagellum. Euglena belongs to a group of animals that move by lashing this whip, and are called Flagellates. The motion of the flagellum also creates a tiny whirlpool that propels tiny particles of food into the little groove that is the Euglena's mouth.

Above, left to right: typhoid bacillus, trypanosome, and vorticella; At right: Euglena

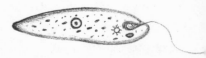

Euglena contains chlorophyll, the green pigment, or coloring matter, found in the leaves and stems of most plants. It enables plants to make food out of water and chemicals in the soil, and out of carbon dioxide in air. By means of chlorophyll Euglena can make its own food. So you can see it can live both as a plant and as an animal. Then, which is it: plant or animal? Scientists say this is an open question.

Usually we have no difficulty in recognizing plants from animals as, for example, in the picture on the next page.

Plants and animals are usually made of millions of cells, although some, like the vorticella, are made of only one cell. The cell is the unit, the smallest living structure that can do all the things that entitle it to be called "living." Cells are blobs of clear protoplasm, or living matter, so small that most can't be seen without a microscope. They differ in size and shape, and in the work they do. But nearly all cells have certain parts in common: a thin membrane, or film, that encloses the clear, thick jelly called protoplasm: a round or oval part, called the nucleus, which is a special kind of protoplasm, necessary for growth and reproduction of the cell; floating

Honey bee on wild strawberry

grains of food and wastes. Sometimes the food and wastes are each in a different bubble-shaped droplet called a vacuole.

Plant and animal cells differ in that the plant has a cell wall made of cellulose—tough, lifeless matter—while animal cells have only a thin film of protoplasm, a living membrane. Fluid and dissolved substances can pass back and forth through the cell membrane of the animal but not through the cell wall of the plant.

Both plants and animals grow. A great many plants continue to grow all their lives. Most animals stop growing when they have reached a certain size.

Plants and animals reproduce themselves: some plants through seeds, and animals in several different ways about which you will read later.

Most plants stay rooted in one place. Ground covers, such as periwinkle *(Vinca minor)*, spread by what is often called "underground roots." But these "roots" are really stems that grow sideways from the main stem, and these form new plants, so that the original plant really hasn't moved. Parts of plants often move, without changing their place. Tulips open in the morning and close at night; stems turn upward and roots downward. When light reaches a plant from one side, the plant moves toward the light. Vine tendrils twine around supports—other plants, a trellis, or a brick wall.

Most animals move about, although some stay in one place throughout their lives. For example, barnacles may stick to the bottom of a ship, clams to a rock, and the Hydra attaches itself to a twig, leaf, or rock, by a disc of cells at its base.

The most important difference between plants and animals is the way they get their food. Most animals, being able to move about, get their food by going after it; plants, being fixed, depend more on themselves.

Most of the world's plants make their own food. These are the green plants familiar to most of us: trees, shrubs, flowers, grasses, and vines. The leaves and stems, with their chlorophyll, are the plants' food-making factories.

Plants get their raw materials from the soil and air; by capturing the energy from the sun they manufacture what they require for their growth. This process is called "photosynthesis."

But mushrooms, molds, bacteria, and yeasts lack chlorophyll, and depend for their food on other plants or even on animals.

Animals do not have chlorophyll. They eat plants and so eat the food made by plants, or get their food from other animals which get it originally from plants. With

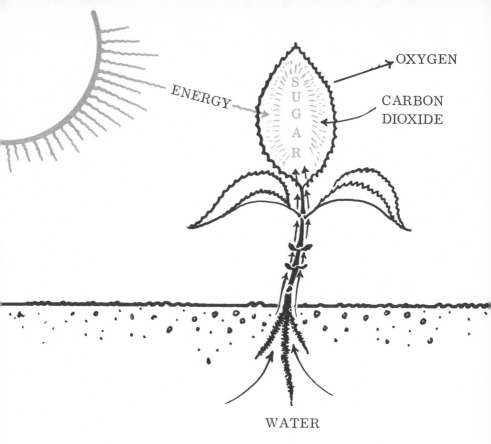

The photosynthesis process

few exceptions, animals have to get their food ready-made.

All living things need energy to live. As we have seen, plants get their energy from the sun. Animals, however, get energy from food. By burning food in their cells, they release the energy that was trapped by the plant in capturing the sun's rays. To burn food, just as to burn coal in a furnace, the cells need oxygen. Animals breathe in air which contains oxygen. They breathe out carbon dioxide. They use oxygen in the same way as a burning candle does; and both give off carbon dioxide. Plants use this carbon dioxide to make more food. While animals breathe continuously, plants make food only when the sun shines. Plants store energy; animals "spend" it all their lives.

Both plants and animals are able to change when their surroundings change. If a potted geranium is hung upside down, its stem will gradually turn upward. If a frog is placed on its back it will quickly right itself. These changes to which plants and animals respond are called stimuli—a sure sign of life. But animals usually respond much faster than plants.

Plants, like animals, are built according to a definite plan of organs and systems with a division of labor for the different parts. For example, as we have said, the leaf is the food-making part of a green plant. The roots hold the plant in place and also provide the means for drawing raw material out of the soil. Some animals have a circulatory system with a heart that pumps blood through blood vessels. All but the simplest animals have sense organs— eyes, ears, taste buds, and organs for touch, smell, and balance—through which they learn about the world around them.

While in many ways the two major groups of living things are both alike and different, plants and animals differ among themselves. There is an orderly grouping of the different kinds in each kingdom.

We separate them by a variety of features: their structure, their level in the scale of life, where they live, how they get food, and by other special characteristics. Simple plants with chlorophyll are classed as algae, while mushrooms, molds, yeasts, and bacteria that lack chlorophyll are classed as fungi. Animals with six walking legs are classed as insects; feathered animals with two legs are birds.

As new animals or plants are discovered or bred, they are studied for all their characteristics; then they are named and placed in the group that they most nearly resemble. The first scientist to discover or breed a new species is given the right to name it. For example, Louis Agassiz, the Swiss-born American scientist, discovered a new kind of American catfish to which he gave the name *Parasilurus aristotelis.* He chose to name it after Aristotle who first described the male Greek catfish's habit of guarding the young. Sometimes fellow scientists name it in honor of the discoverer. An example is a marsh grass discovered in 1870 at Southhampton, England. It was named *Spartina townsendii* in honor of Frederick Townsend, who recognized it as a new species.

Mushrooms: fungi

Red algae

4

THE WORLD
OF PLANTS

Biologists agree on four main groups or phyla of plants. They are divided mainly according to complexity—from the simplest to the most complex—and from the oldest to the newest as they have evolved. The four phyla are: Thallophyte, Bryophyte, Pteridophyte, and Spermatophyte. These long and unfamiliar names really help to identify a plant by its special features. Phyte means plant, and the first part of the word describes its type.

STEMLESS AND ROOTLESS

The Thallophytes were probably the first living things on earth; therefore they are the oldest and simplest of plants. Thallus is the Greek word for young shoot. Thallophytes have no stems, leaves, or roots. There are many thousands of species in this group; yet they are not as familiar to us as elms or cabbages. Some consist of a single cell, and others grow to many feet in length, but all have a primitive structure compared with other plants. Under modern high-power microscopes, they may be more complicated than was previously believed. For example, when enlarged a thousand times, they appear to have a circulatory system.

Thallophytes are in two subphyla: algae and fungi.

GREEN FOOD FOR WHALES

Algae contain chlorophyll and therefore can live independently. Nearly all algae are water plants. Since they have no roots, they cannot get moisture from the soil, and can live only when immersed in water or when covered by a watery film. A few grow on tree trunks, but only during rainy spells.

Algae are further grouped by their color: blue-green, green, brown, and red. The Red Sea got its name because it contains so much red algae that the water appears to be red. Seaweed—algae that grow in long strips—may be all the colors of the rainbow. Some species of algae, the diatoms, form glass-like shells around themselves. They are so pretty that they are called the "jewels" of the plant kingdom. In fresh-water ponds algae furnish food for many fish, and in the ocean these tiny plants, along with floating and swimming animalcules (miniature animals), make up plankton—food for the giant blue whale, and other creatures of the sea.

Diatoms in water

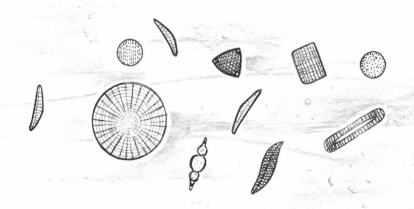

Plankton in the ocean

PLANTS WITHOUT COLOR

There are almost as many different kinds of fungi as there are of algae. Because they lack chlorophyll they live off living things, or once living things. Among the fungi are the bacteria, yeasts and molds, mushrooms, toadstools (which are poisonous mushrooms), rusts and smuts (which cause diseases of plants), and mildews. Fungi that get their food from once living things, or what is called dead organic matter, are harmless. Fungi that live in or on other living things are called parasites. Disease-producing bacteria are typical parasites, damaging or killing animals and people. The smuts and rusts live on wheat, rye, and corn, destroying these crops.

Bread mold is not a true parasite because bread is not a living thing. From one species of bread mold we get

penicillin, though not all species of bread mold are useful.

Bacteria that live on decayed plants or humus, dead animals, garbage, and sewage have important uses for people. By breaking down the dead matter they release food for themselves, but they also release the chemicals that go into the making of new living things. Some bacteria and molds turn milk into cheese and give cheeses their special flavors. Yeast leavens bread, making it spongy, and ferments fruit juices into wine and other alcoholic beverages. Certain bacteria change cabbage into sauerkraut and give the flavor to pickles and green olives; others produce juices that turn stored crops into cattle feed.

But some fungi are not so useful. Some mushrooms we eat, while toadstools contain deadly poison. Mildew, another fungus, is damaging in another way. By its strange appetite for leather and for animal and vegetable fibers it destroys shoes and clothing.

Common mushroom   **Toadstool (Fly Amanita)**

  Below is an interesting member of the Thallophytes—
the lichens. These grow on rocks and logs, and are made
up of threads of a fungus plant containing one-celled
algae. The algae make food for the fungi. The fungi break
down the rock, releasing the chemicals for the algae, and
the algae furnish the fungi with food. Thus they live in
a neighborly partnership which is helpful to both. This
type of arrangement between two living things is called
"symbiosis" meaning "harmonious living."

Lichen on rock   **Closeup of lichen**

MANY-CELLED PLANTS

Mosses and liverworts are Bryophytes, more highly organized because they contain many cells. Their name comes from the Greek word meaning "sprouting leaf." They have stems and delicate leaves with chlorophyll, so that they can make their own food. But they do not have either roots or flowers. Instead they have cells that penetrate the soil; these anchor the plant and absorb raw materials from the soil, but are not real roots. They have no woody supporting parts, and therefore never grow tall.

Liverworts are the simplest land plants. They have a many-celled structure that is anchored by hair-like projections into the ground or a log.

The mosses and liverworts produce eggs and sperms (female and male cells); when these unite they develop into spores and, scattered by the wind, start new plants.

Peat mosses grow in hollows containing still water. They grow inward from the side of the bog until they form a floating mass of plant material. New moss continually grows on the old moss which dies. This process continues until the hollow is filled. The lower layers decay, forming carbon. If left undisturbed for hundreds of thousands of years the moss turns into coal beds. Peat moss is often used to enrich the soil for house plants and gardens. And in some countries the peat moss (before it becomes carbon) is often packed into blocks and used as fuel. You have probably heard of the peat bogs of Ireland.

ENTER THE FERNS

The phylum Pteridophyte, from the Greek word for

Peat moss in a bog

fern, consists of green plants. They are more highly developed than the mosses, because in addition to leaves and stems (which are woody) they have true roots. But they do not have flowers. Ferns vary in size from tiny plants less than an inch long to some six feet tall. The plants' woody stems and roots help to carry more water and enable these ferns to grow tall. At one time in the earth's history the ferns were very numerous and flourished in a great many parts of the world. Later, many ferns died out; conditions were more favorable for the seed-bearing plants. In the same way, the giant and awkward dinosaurs gave way to the modern reptiles.

Since ferns have neither flowers nor seeds, they grow by spores on the undersurface of the leaf. They are all perennial, which means that they grow year after year, while plants that are called "annuals" live for only one growing season. Boston fern, Christmas fern, and maidenhair fern are true ferns.

There are also horsetails which differ from true ferns because their leaves are small and underdeveloped; most of the photosynthesis occurs in stems. Horsetails grow in sandy places and even in cinders along railroad tracks.

Then there are the club mosses which are not mosses at all because they have the specialized structure of all Pteridophytes, and true mosses, as you know, are all Bryophytes. Club mosses grow on the floor of the forest. Their many-branching, trailing stems are green, and, like the leaves, can make food.

THE SEED-BEARERS

The fourth group of plants, and the most highly developed, are the Spermatophytes. In addition to root,

Left: Boston fern; Center: Christmas fern and spores; Right: Maidenhair fern

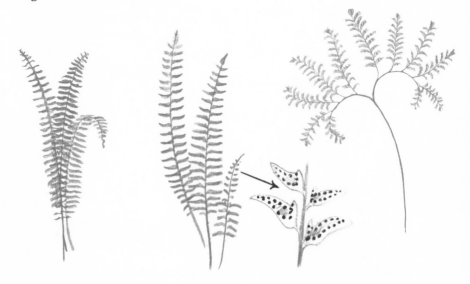

Horsetails in cinders on railroad track

stem, and leaf, they have flowers—the seed-producing parts from which the name "sperm" comes, meaning seed. Most plants that come to your mind are likely to be seed-bearers—trees and shrubs, vines and grasses, and all the flowering plants. Reproduction by seeds is the farthest plants have gone in the process of evolution.

The seed plants are the most numerous. They have almost taken over the land. One reason why they have flourished to this extent is that they possess a pollen tube. This organ makes possible the transference of the sperm to the egg without the need for water. As a result, these

Club mosses on floor of forest

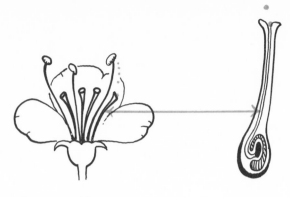

Pollen tube of seed-bearer

plants have been able to reproduce in a variety of ways and places.

NAKED AND ENCLOSED SEEDS

The seed-bearers are divided into two large classes: those whose seeds are exposed (Gymnosperms), and those whose seeds are formed inside a fruit (Angiosperms). However else an oak or a maple differs from a pine or a cedar, to the biologist the true difference that separates them into two classes is the way they bear seeds.

White oak with acorn; white pine with exposed seeds

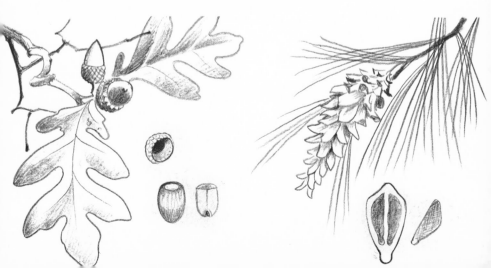

The most numerous and familiar Gymnosperms are the conifers or cone-bearers—spruce, fir, pine, and cedar trees. These are the evergreens with needle-like leaves and cones. These trees develop two kinds of cones. One is the male cone that produces pollen grains which contain the sperm; the other is the female cone which contains the eggs. The male cones release the pollen which is scattered by the wind, falling onto the female cones.

The needle-like leaves lose little water during the summer heat, do not freeze in winter, and withstand the force of storms. Because they do not shed their leaves in winter, they are called "ever"-green.

Other Gymnosperm orders are the cycads, with large divided fern-like or palm-like leaves; the ginkgo, with fan-shaped leaves, and the tropical gnetales. These are decorative plants only, while the conifers have practical uses in addition to being beautiful. Their wood is used for inexpensive furniture, for paper, and for the making of plastics. A gummy substance, called resin, secreted by

White pine cones—(left) male; (right) female

special canals in the tree, makes tar, oils, and turpentine. But the one thing they all have in common, that gives them the name Gymnosperm, is their seed-bearing cones.

The Angiosperms are the true flowering plants. Their seeds develop inside a closed ovary which is part of the fruit. They are the most numerous plants. There are probably as many as 150,000 different species varying in size, shape, habitat; some are even partly or wholly parasitic. The orchid and the mistletoe, for example, have little chlorophyll, and so live on other plants. A few Angiosperms, strangely, eat small animals. The flytrap plant, with white leaves, secretes a sticky substance to which insects are attracted. When the insect alights on the plant, the leaf closes on it and digests it.

But what distinguishes all of them is that they develop flowers and fruits. The flower contains the sex parts: the stamen is the male part and carries the pollen; the pistil, through which the pollen tube grows, extending down to the ovary, is the female part. When the egg is fertilized

Venus flytrap plant, open and closed

inside the ovary, the fruit is formed. The fruit contains the seeds from which the new plant grows.

You can trace the way all this happens by following the arrows in the picture.

The Angiosperms are further divided into two groups called subclasses, the monocotyledons and the dicotyle-

Fertilization process

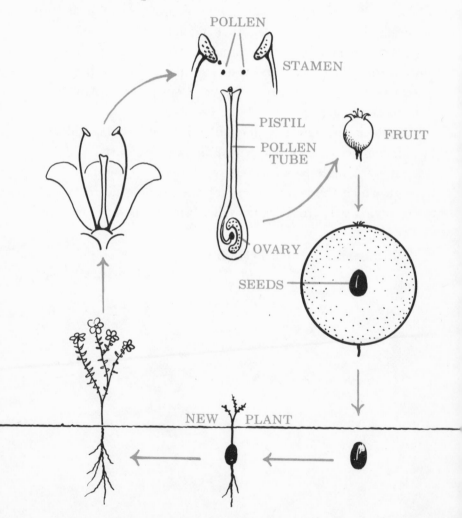

Left: Swamp buttercup; Center: Wild yellow lily; Right: Iris

dons. The monocot seed has one embryo (the developing seed) leaf, or cotyledon, and the dicot seed has two cotyledons. The leaves in the mature monocot plant have parallel veins and smooth edges. (You will remember that l'Obel put these plants in one class because of the shape of their leaves.) In the dicots the leaves branch, and their edges are usually indented. There are other differences in the stems and flower parts that you can see in the picture.

At the top of this page and on the next two pages are some familiar plants that belong to the Angiosperms. Can you arrange them according to the subclasses of monocots and dicots?

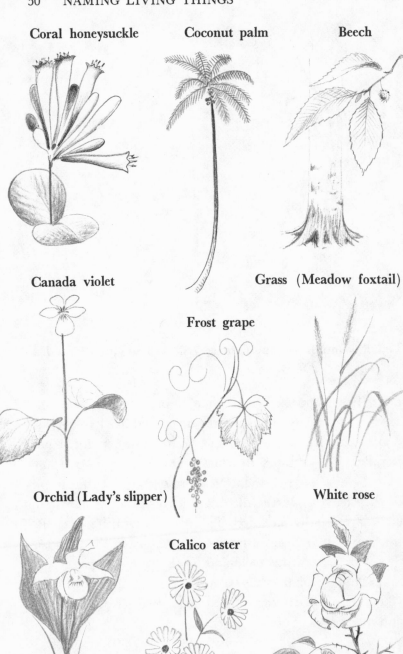

Coral honeysuckle

Coconut palm

Beech

Canada violet

Grass (Meadow foxtail)

Frost grape

Orchid (Lady's slipper)

Calico aster

White rose

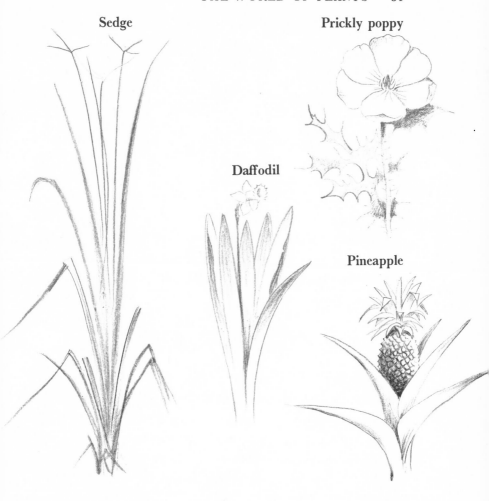

Sedge

Prickly poppy

Daffodil

Pineapple

ANSWER

Monocots		Dicots	
grass	lily	buttercup	poppy
palm	sedge	rose	grape
orchid	pineapple	violet	aster
iris	daffodil	beech	honeysuckle

Big brown bat

5

BACKBONE OR NOT?

We know that Aristotle divided all animals into two broad groups, and that Lamarck called these groups invertebrates and vertebrates. Today we divide the animal kingdom into ten phyla. The near-million members of the ten phyla range from the simplest one-celled animals to man.

LIKENESSES AND DIFFERENCES

How is this vast array of animals catalogued? Often, what may seem to us striking differences are only surface distinctions to the biologist, rather than differences in basic plan. And features that, to us, seem closely related are really far apart. Birds and bats both fly, but are very different in structure and belong on different levels in the scale of life. The whale swims, but is much more closely related to a cow than a fish.

Size does not put animals into different groups. The mouse is a closer relative of the elephant or the whale than of the frog. It is still more closely related to the muskrat, prairie dog, and beaver—all of them being rodents.

The wing of a bird and of a butterfly serve the same

function, but are structurally very different. On the other hand, the arm of man, the wing of a bird, and the front fin of a fish are closely linked as limbs which evolved from one basic structure—the pectoral or breast appendage— but each is adapted for a specialized use.

LIFE IN A DROP OF POND SCUM

If you place a drop of water from a stagnant pool under the microscope, you are likely to find an assortment of creatures: an Ameba, a Paramecium, a Stentor, a water-flea, a sow bug, a Euglena, and perhaps a Planarian (flatworm). These seven animals fall into three different phyla, relatively far apart in the animal scale.

We now begin the slow and steady march in evolution from the lowest to the highest forms.

PROTOZOA

All the thousands of species of Protozoa are single-celled. You already know that Euglena belongs to the Protozoa. The Paramecium, the Ameba, and the Stentor are also protozoans. They are alike in that they are composed of only one cell, but because of their differences they belong in different classes of this phylum.

The Ameba is constantly changing its shape. By a slow, crawling motion, part of its mass oozes in the direction of a particle of food, or draws back before a threatening stimulus. This extension is called a pseudopod, or false foot. Its type of motion puts it into the class of Sarcodina.

The slipper-shaped Paramecium is covered with per-

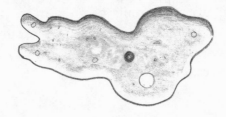

Ameba

haps 2,500 hair-like projections of protoplasm called cilia. Cilia in motion, like so many oars, propel the animal in a swimming movement. When the cilia are cut off, the animal becomes motionless, but with them it can dart forward, back up, or turn around. The Paramecium belongs to the class of Ciliates.

The Stentor also has cilia, but under the microscope you can see that these encircle only the wide end, where they sweep food into its "gullet." The other end is stalked and anchored, perhaps to a leaf.

Then there are the Flagellates, such as the Euglena, which move by the whiplashing motion of the long, thread-like flagellum. (See page 29.)

Now watch the creeping motion of the flatworm (see page 59). On its undersurface it has cilia which only partly account for its crawl. Both the Ameba and the

Paramecium

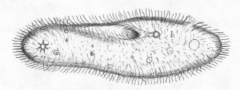

Stentor

flatworm are crawlers, but how far apart they are in the animal tree! You will discover this when we talk about worms.

Daphnia, or the water-flea, and the sow bug are still more advanced and belong with the lobster, crab, and barnacle in a phylum which will be described later.

PORIFERA—THE SPONGES

In the world of nature, changes take place exceedingly slowly. After the Protozoa came the sponges, many-celled animals. Instead of one cell having to carry on all the life functions, we find the beginning of a division of labor. Some cells feed the body, and others support or reproduce it. The scientific name of the phylum—Porifera—means "pore-bearer." Sponges are living strainers: water and tiny plants and animals enter the pores; some pores strain out the food, while others throw off the wastes. The inner wall is lined with cells bearing flagella; by their constant lashing they create a current which carries oxygen-containing water to the cells, and carbon dioxide away from the cells.

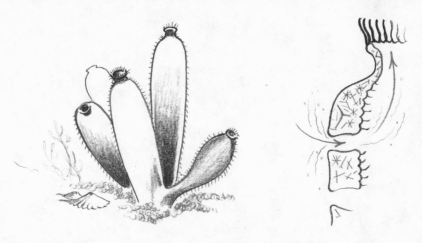

Sponge, showing inner wall, with cells and flagella

There are as yet no organs such as a heart or brain, and therefore no coordination between the cells; these are more like independent units fused into one animal.

HOLLOW INSIDE: THE COELENTERATES

The next development is the formation of a hollow in animals with a body cavity. These are the Coelenterates, which means "hollow gut." The interior of the hollow sac is a digestive cavity with an opening at one end that serves as a mouth.

The Hydra, a tiny animal that lives in ponds, is a typical Coelenterate. Under the microscope you can see the double layer of cells that encloses the central cavity, its combined digestive tract and supply system. When seen with the naked eye, it looks more like a bit of frayed string, each strand being a tentacle. It got its name from the Greek myth. Hercules, the Greek god, fought the monster Hydra by cutting off one of its heads, only to find that

Hydra

two new ones grew in its place. The real Hydra, which is about half an inch long, can also be cut into several pieces, and each piece will grow into a whole animal.

What is new in the Coelenterates is the double-layered wall of cells. The outer layer of cells makes a protective covering. The inner layer contains the first epithelial cells (like the smooth cells that line your mouth and digestive tract). In the Hydra, these cells digest food. This animal also has the beginnings of muscle cells. By means of such elongated structures the Hydra can contract or expand— shortening, lengthening, or bending its soft body.

These primitive animals are also the first to have true nerve cells; these make up a loose, irregular network that coordinates the work of the tentacles, the muscles, and gland cells.

The Hydra has many Coelenterate cousins: the jelly-fish, sea anemone, coral, the Portuguese man-of-war, and others. The tentacles of the last may be fifty feet long. The tip of each of these long "arms" is equipped with stinging capsules that can paralyze a large fish or even inflict a serious wound on a man.

ALL KINDS OF WORMS

Next in the animal parade are three phyla of worms: flatworms, roundworms, and segmented or *true* worms.

What's new about flatworms, such as the Planaria which you can fish out of any pond or spring? They are many-celled animals belonging to the lowest phylum of worms. They have arrow-shaped heads and pointed tails. Like the Hydra, flatworms have a common digestive and circulatory cavity, with the mouth opening at one end. But the flatworm has a third or middle layer of cells: an outer covering, an inner lining, and a middle layer in between. It has a body cavity and several simple organs. A muscular pharynx, or throat, for taking in food, eye-spots near the head end, and male and female reproductive organs make it a more highly organized animal. In its crawling movements it uses not only cilia but also muscle cells.

It also has a special organ not seen in lower animal forms. This is a network of fine tubes which develop from the middle layer. Through these tubes the flatworm gets rid of its waste—the beginnings of a kidney! Another new structure is a simple nervous system—a brain at the head end, and nerves that run from the head to the tail end.

Planaria are non-parasitic animals, sometimes feeding on vegetation or on Hydra. But their relatives—the flukes and tapeworms—are parasites. Liver flukes feed on fish, cattle, and in some parts of the world they cause human disease, attacking the liver.

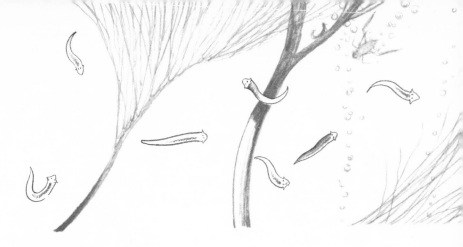

Planaria (flatworm)

The tapeworm is a long, flat, ribbon-like animal. Tapeworms get into the intestines of many vertebrates, including man. The head end of the worm is equipped with suckers and a circle of hooks. With these hooks the worm attaches itself to the lining of the intestine, absorbing much of the food of the host, the animal to which it is attached. Unlike the other flatworms, the tapeworm does not have its own digestive system; it feeds on the digested materials it soaks up from the intestinal canal of its victim.

Tapeworm

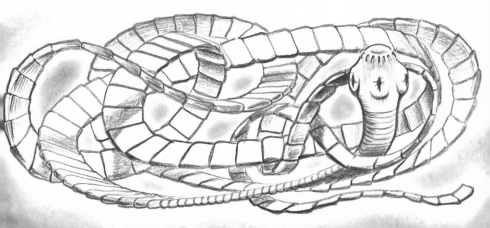

The next phylum consists of three classes of round-worms, nearly all parasitic. They are found almost anywhere—in the soil, in the ocean, lake, or pond, and even in drinking water. They have soft, threadlike bodies pointed at both ends. They literally "worm" their way into the body. The hookworm is one of the most damaging, piercing the skin of people who walk barefoot in fields. One roundworm called Ascaris grows in the throat of the horse, and another, the trichina worm, infects hogs. When infected pork is not cooked long enough, the embryos or eggs get into the intestine of man, pass undigested through the blood, and burrow their way into the muscles. There the eggs develop into the next stage called "larvae"— worm-like bodies. In this way they cause trichinosis, a disease of the muscles in man.

The roundworms have not only a digestive tract, but

Left: Ascaris; Center: Hookworm; Right: Trichina in muscle

also a separate circulatory system which consists of muscular tubes. Here we find also the first blood cells.

So far, we have read about half of the ten phyla mentioned at the beginning of this chapter: Protozoa, Porifera, Coelenterates, flatworms, and roundworms. And we have still not placed all of the seven animals in that one drop of water!

The sixth phylum—Annelida, the true worms—contains the familiar earthworm, which has a ringed or segmented body. The series of segments represents an advance in evolution, each segment being one unit of the body. The body of true worms is made of two cylindrical tubes, one inside the other. The outer one is the body wall, and the inner tube its digestive tract. This digestive system shows several advances over that of other worms: it contains in addition to a muscular pharynx, a gullet, and a double stomach—a thin-walled crop for storing food and, behind it, a thick-walled muscular gizzard for grinding it into tiny bits. It also has an intestine and a rectum.

Its circulatory system is more complicated. Two long blood vessels with many branches to the segments distribute the blood. Also, in the region of the gullet the two vessels are connected by pairs of muscular tubes called "hearts." The system for discharging wastes has paired organs repeated in almost every segment of the body.

The nervous system also is different. It contains a large two-lobed group of nerve cells just above the pharynx, and another just below it. The lower ganglion (group of nerve cells) is connected with a nerve cord whose fibers extend to every segment. The earthworm is equipped with muscles which are stimulated when danger threatens. As the muscles contract the worm draws its body back into the earth.

The earthworm is a friend of the farmer. It helps to break up the soil and turn it over.

Other members of the annelids are the sandworms, clamworms, and bloodworms, marine relatives of the earthworm. These make fishermen's bait. The leeches are annelids, too. They are parasitic, blood-sucking worms with suckers at both ends. The glands that produce saliva in the leech also produce a chemical that prevents the blood from clotting while the animal is feeding.

STARFISHES AND SEA-URCHINS

Next come the Echinoderms, a group of marine animals built like wheels or stars. The skin of these creatures

Left: Earthworm; Center: Sandworm; Right: Leech

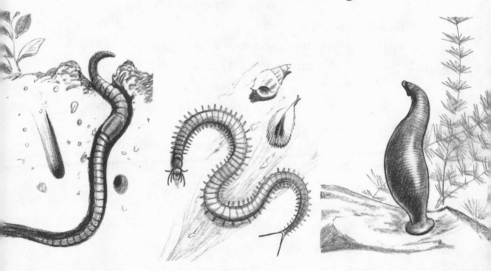

Starfish

is rough and covered with spiny projections, which gives them their name, meaning "hedgehog-skinned." The starfish has rows of tube feet on the arms or rays. It feeds on the soft bodies of oysters and clams. Wrapping its rays around its prey, it pulls at the oyster shell with a steady pull that pries it open.

The stomach of the starfish is on the undersurface of the body. It has a strange way of getting its food. It pushes its stomach out through its mouth. The starfish wraps its stomach around the soft body of the clam, which it then digests. After that it draws its stomach back into its body.

The sea-urchin, which looks like a pincushion, lives close to the shore of the ocean. To protect itself from the pounding waves, it grinds holes in rocks into which it crawls for concealment. The sea-urchins and sand-dollars have a wheel shape like starfish, but their spines and tube feet are shorter. You find the dried shells of sand-dollars on the beach, and you can see how they got their names from their round shape with "engraved" markings.

Other relatives are the sea-cucumbers, the sluggish-moving, leathery-skinned animals that resemble a cucumber. Sea-lilies are nearly extinct relatives. Their branching feather rays look a little like a feather duster on a stalk. Most of these are known to us as fossils, remains of creatures from a distant past.

Top left: Sea-urchin; Top right: Sand-dollar; Lower left: Sea-cucumber; Lower right: Sea-lilies

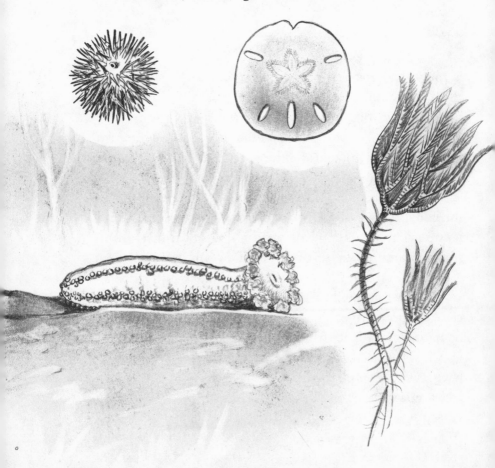

6

TOP RUNG
OF THE
SOFT-BODIED

At the top of the invertebrate world are two phyla more complex than the seven earlier ones we have just been talking about. A great many of these creatures are at times considered severe competitors to the human race. Some attack man's food supply, and others bring disease to cattle and people. Because of these threats, they must be kept under constant check.

WITH AND WITHOUT SHELLS

The phylum Mollusca is the second largest of all animal phyla. Since evolution proceeded not only from the simpler to the more complex but also by offshooting branches, it is possible that the worms and the molluscs had a common ancestor, the worms developing along a segmental plan, like the annelids, and the molluscs on a unique body plan without segmentation.

The molluscs include oysters, clams, octopuses, snails, slugs, and the largest of all invertebrates, the giant squid. The main features that distinguish this phylum are: a broad, flat, muscular foot for creeping along rocks and for anchoring when the animal is disturbed; a mantle or

Slug

fold of tissue that covers the internal organs and laps over the edges of the foot; a hard shell made of lime, produced by the upper surface of the mantle. The shell gives protection, but it hinders motion. But all molluscs do not have all of these features.

The snails, limpets, and whelks—the Gastropods, or belly-footed—have a single shell, often coiled into a spiral. The slugs, which belong in this group, have no shell at all or, at most, a remnant of one.

Snail

A second class, called the bivalves, have two shells joined by a hinge, and kept tight shut by powerful muscles. Oysters, clams, scallops, and mussels are the best-known bivalves. They are known to us chiefly because they make good food. The shells of the clam show lines of growth, and the number of these parallel markings increases with the age of the animal.

The most highly developed of the molluscs is the squid,

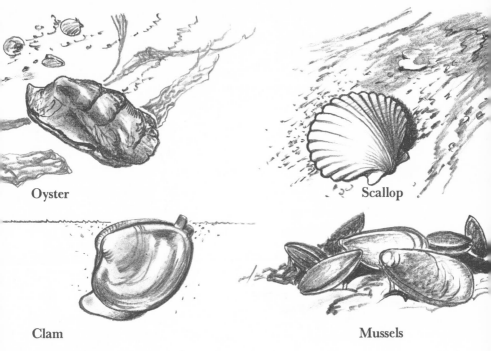

Oyster

Scallop

Clam

Mussels

which is a Cephalopod. It has two large, well-developed eyes. Some of this class that inhabit the depths of the sea are studded with lighting organs which act as lanterns. Giant squid grow to be more than fifty feet long. The squid is equipped to move very rapidly. It throws out a jet of sea water, which causes it to dart backwards. The squid also has an ink sac through which it discharges an inky black cloud in front of itself. This camouflages the squid so it can escape from its enemies. (See next page.)

The octopus, like the squid, uses a jet of water, whose sudden discharge propels the animal backward. To move forward, it uses eight long arms with a double row of sucking disks on each arm. Its inky camouflage colors the sur-

Squid

face of its body with different hues—pink, yellow, brown, and black.

The digestive system of the molluscs consists of a single tube which is often coiled. In this tube are a mouth, throat, gullet, stomach, intestine, and an anus through which the wastes leave. The circulatory system contains a primitive heart pumping blood through a system of branched vessels. Below the heart there are two organs for extracting wastes from the blood. Molluscs have two pairs of nerve cords, one going to the foot and the other to the mantle. Except for the squids and octopuses, molluscs lack the well-developed sense organs. They depend on their shells for protection.

Clams and oysters get their food by straining sea water carried in by the organ called a siphon. The water passes over the gills and is kept in motion by the beating of cilia on their surface. Squids, nautiluses, and octopuses are predatory animals, seizing and holding their prey by long tentacles that are covered with suckers.

ARMOR AND JOINTED LEGS

Last in the procession of the soft-bodied animals are the Arthropoda. The name means paired, jointed legs.

Their bodies are segmented, like those of worms, but all have outer shields, called exoskeletons. An exoskeleton is no more like your skeleton and mine than is a coat of armor. And that's what it is—a suit of armor (in sections) for better defense and protection of the soft insides.

This hard, stiff armor is dead matter secreted by living epithelial cells, and deposited in three layers: the outer layer is waxy and waterproof, the middle one rigid, and the inner layer is made of a stiff substance, called "chitin," which resembles the cellulose of plants. The exoskeleton restricts movement and growth. To grow, the animal sheds its protective coat every now and then, a process called molting; during that time it is open to attack. The rigid

Crayfish molting

layer is thinner over the joints of the legs and between the body segments, and so, with the help of powerful muscles, some of these animals can move over long distances.

The biologists tell us that Arthropods are the most successful of all animals. They are considered successful because there are more species in the Arthropod phylum than there are in all other phyla put together. Arthropods are all over the world, living in many kinds of homes. They reproduce in many different ways, and what a variety of menus they enjoy! The hundreds of thousands of species in this phylum differ as much as a lobster differs from a butterfly, yet they are all divided into four classes by one characteristic: the number of paired legs.

The millipedes and centipedes are many-legged, although they never have as many as the thousand or even hundred legs that you would expect from their names.

The lobsters, crayfish, shrimp, waterbugs, and barnacles have ten legs; spiders, scorpions, and ticks eight, and insects six. People often call spiders insects, but you can see they are not.

Lobsters and crayfish use their legs as paddles for swimming. Barnacles which, as adults, settle down to a life on ship bottoms or wooden dock pilings, use their legs to get food. Their feathery feet whip plankton into their mouths. The millipede uses its legs in a slow crawl, and the horseshoe crab catches sand worms and molluscs with pincer-like legs. Many insects walk and jump with their legs.

And now for the characteristics that separate each kind into its special class.

ARMOR AND CLAW

We've come a long way to reach the last of the animals we found in that drop of water! Water-fleas and sow bugs, along with lobsters, crabs, crayfish, barnacles, and shrimp, are crustaceans. The head and thorax (chest) are fused into one. Most of them live in water—the lobster in the sea and the crayfish in fresh water, for example. All breathe with gills.

Let's look at the lobster for the crustacean body plan. In its stomach it has horny teeth that tear up its food. It has a digestive gland. A heart pumps blood into the body spaces. It has green, kidney-like glands that get rid of liquid wastes, and an anus that disposes of solid particles. It has two pairs of antennae for feeling, one eye for seeing, and a long nerve cord with bead-like enlargements on it made of a cluster of nerve cells, and a brain. The front-

Lobster, showing crustacean body plan

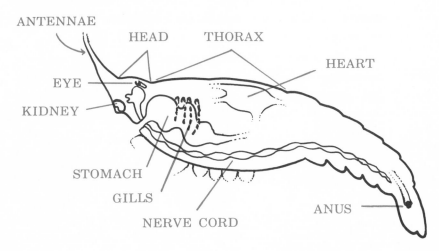

most of the walking legs are giant pincers—one for holding and one for crushing. The fertilized eggs are carried in a brood-pouch until they form larvae. These swim away.

The water-flea—Daphnia—and the sow bug are scavengers, living on decayed plants and animals; the hermit crab makes its home in the shell of a mollusc; the copepod, tiniest of crustaceans, is the most important of foods for fish; the sand-colored ghost crab lives on the beach and is hard to find against the sand. But all are crustaceans in their main body structure.

PLENTY OF LEGS

At first glance the two classes—millipedes and centipedes—look like worms, but their jointed legs, exoskeletons, and complicated internal organs put them into the Arthropod phylum. The centipedes have one pair of legs on each body segment. Their small claws produce a poison that paralyzes the insects, earthworms, and even the lizards that they eat. The millipedes have two pairs of legs on each segment, and use them to crawl in a rhythmic, wave-like motion. When in danger they wind up in a

Left: Daphnia; Center: Sow bug; Right: Hermit crab

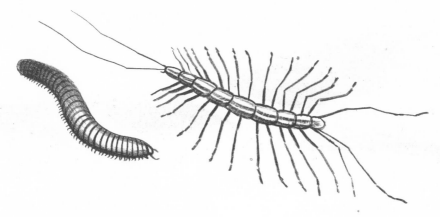

Left: Millipede; Right: Centipede

tight coil, with the soft underside protected by their armor. They eat decayed vegetation.

THE STRANGE RELATIVES OF
THE SPIDER

The class of Arachnida are mostly land-bound, use their eight legs for walking, have eight eyes, and breathe with what are called "book lungs." Their name means "web." There are the spiders, only some of which spin webs, including the trapdoor spider which digs a hole in the ground, lines it with silk, and closes it with a hinged leg. The scorpions live in the tropics, hide by day, and hunt insects by night. The ticks pierce the skin of animals and gorge themselves with blood. There are the mites that cause diseases of leaves, and others that burrow into animal and human skins. And a yet stranger relative is the king or horseshoe crab, sometimes called a "living fossil" because there are only a few species alive today. He is called a crab, but is not a crustacean.

Scorpion

Trapdoor spider

Tick

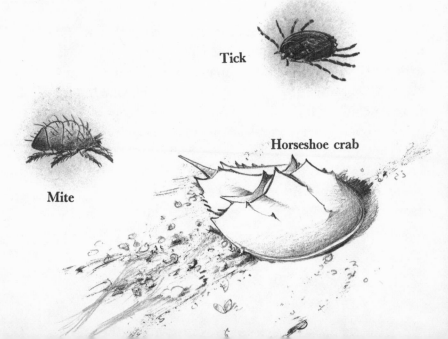

Horseshoe crab

Mite

Deer fly

Cucumber beetle

Grasshopper

INSECTS—WHAT A CLASS FOR SIZE

No class is as large as the insects, and in appearance they are astonishingly varied. Twenty-four orders have been described to account for all their types and differences. But all have three pairs of legs, and a segmented body divided into three parts—the head, thorax, and abdomen. The head usually carries a pair of antennae, complicated eyes, and heavy jaws that work sideways.

Insects are the only invertebrates that have developed wings, though some are wingless. Most have two pairs. The fly has one pair for flying, and one pair for balancing. Grasshoppers and beetles have stiffened protective structures. These are made of chitin, they are flexible enough to allow movement, rigid for protection, and are waterproof besides. They breathe through branching air tubes or tracheas, and those that spend part of their early life in water have gill-like equipment.

Insects reproduce by going through definite stages. Their complicated life history is called metamorphosis, which means body change. The butterfly lays eggs on a leaf, the eggs hatch not into butterflies but into caterpillars or larvae. The caterpillar spins a silk thread with the spinneret under its mouth, and turns into a pupa, a resting

Metamorphosis of Monarch butterfly

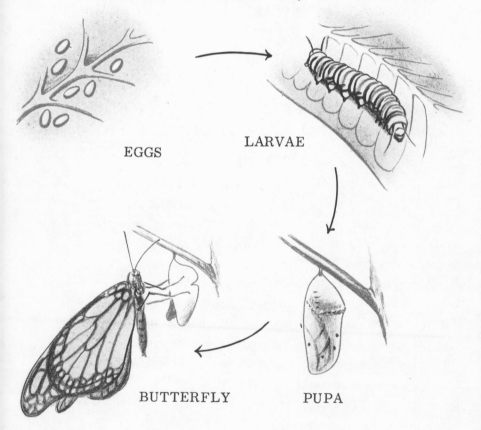

EGGS   LARVAE

BUTTERFLY   PUPA

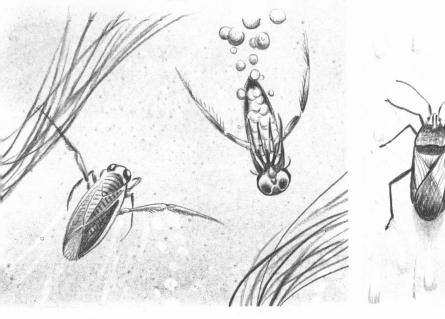

Left: Water boatman; Right: Back-swimmer   **Squash bug**

stage. Inside the pupa case, which is formed from the larval skin, a complete transformation takes place. Then the butterfly emerges without any resemblance to either the pupa or larva.

Most of the insects that are familiar to us belong in eight different orders. Would you think that the grasshopper and the cockroach are in the same order? Together with katydids, crickets, walking sticks, and praying mantises they are all straight-winged, and have chewing mouths that feed mainly on plants.

Then there are the beetles, weevils, and fireflies. This largest group of insects have one important structure in common: the front wings form a horny sheath which covers the second folded, thin pair of wings.

You have heard all kinds of creatures called "bugs," including bacteria. The biologist gives the name of *true bug* to only one order of insects. Here are some of them: water boatmen, back-swimmers, squash bugs, and bed-bugs. They have thickened, leathery front wings, and piercing-sucking mouths. Some, like the chinch bug and squash bug, damage crops. Bedbugs are wingless species that live on animal (usually human) blood, and the giant waterbug and water scorpion (not a scorpion at all) have a biting sting. In metamorphosis they skip the pupal stage.

Flies, mosquitoes, and gnats have one pair of wings and a pair of knobbed balancing organs. They are among the most pestiferous of insects with biting, sucking mouths. Some carry disease: the anopheles and aedes mosquitoes spread malaria and yellow fever, and the housefly, with-out biting, spreads germs.

Butterflies and moths belong to the same order, but here is how you can tell them apart. Both have rigid wings covered with overlapping scales that give them their color, but on butterfly wings the scales are flat, on moths, hair-like. Butterflies fly in the daytime and their feelers have knobs at the tip; moths fly at night and usually their feelers are feathery. In the resting position, a moth has its wings spread, and a butterfly folds its wings.

The coddling moth, corn borer, and tent caterpillar damage our crops. The silkworm moth cocoon, which is the pupa stage, is unwound to make silk.

Termites, tunneling into wood

QUEEN   DRONE   WORKER

EGG   LARVAE

Beehive, showing queen, drone, worker, egg, and larvae

Termites make up yet another order of wood-eating insects that are often called house-wreckers. They avoid light and they tunnel their way into wood, wearing down solid posts into hollow, weakened tubes. The curious thing is that they cannot digest the wood without help. Protozoa that live in the termite's digestive tract work over the cellulose so that the termite can digest it.

Ants, bees, and wasps have thin membrane wings. They go through complete metamorphosis, and most of them live in elaborate communities in which a division of labor is the rule of their tribe. Among the bees there are the drones. These are males, "born" from eggs that have not been fertilized, that is, in which sperm cells took no part; infertile females who are workers; and the queen, the only fertile female, that can produce young. The larvae produced by the queen are fed "royal jelly," secreted by the glands of workers. Ants also live in social colonies,

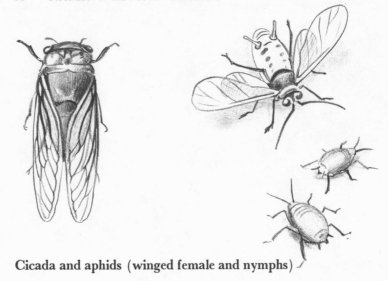

Cicada and aphids (winged female and nymphs)

and while their behavior seems remarkable to us, they follow certain unlearned habits which they inherit at "birth."

The cicadas, aphids, leaf hoppers, and scales make up another order with sucking mouth parts. Most are serious crop damagers.

When you think of the name "insect" and the myriads of different kinds there are, you see what an enormous job it is to unscramble them and catalogue the class by order, family, genus, and species.

Here are pictures of a snail, a giant squid, an abalone, an oyster, an octopus, a scallop, and a clam. These are alike because they are all soft-bodied, unsegmented animals. Since they all have a muscular foot and a mantle, they are molluscs. Scientists put them in three classes by their differences. Can you group them by these differences?

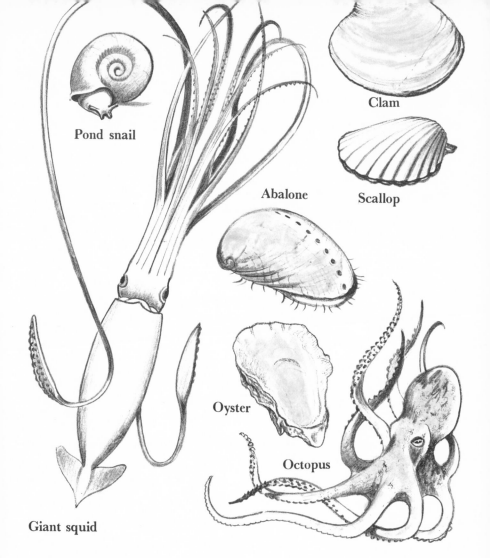

Pond snail

Clam

Scallop

Abalone

Oyster

Octopus

Giant squid

ANSWER

The abalone and snail have a coiled shell; therefore they are Gastropods or belly-footed molluscs.

The oyster, clam, and scallop are bivalves with double hinged shells.

The octopus and squid are Cephalopods, related by their grasping organs or tentacles.

7

ENTER
THE
BACKBONE

Sea lamprey

Here comes the tenth and last great phylum of animals —Chordata. The name stands for the notochord, a supporting rod of cartilage (gristle), which is the forerunner of the spinal column. The chordates also have a hollow nerve cord and gill slits at some stage in their development.

A small division of the chordates includes some lowly creatures such as the sea squirts and lampreys that form the link between the soft-bodied invertebrates and the vertebrates. In these animals the notochord is an elastic single stiff rod that runs along the axis of the body.

All vertebrates, from fish to man, have certain structures in common. They have a jointed backbone which encloses and protects the spinal cord, and a skull containing a brain linked with the spinal cord. At the other end of the spinal column there is some sort of tail, long in some, short in others and, in man, the bare remains of a tail completely hidden inside the body. All vertebrates have some organs for breathing, red blood cells, a heart, a liver, a pancreas, spleen, kidneys, and organs of reproduction.

The five familiar classes of the vertebrate subphylum are: fish, amphibians, reptiles, birds, and mammals.

WHAT MAKES A FISH A FISH?

Fishes are backboned, finned animals that live in water and breathe with gills. The water may be salty, fresh, brackish, or muddy, cold or tropically warm. Some kinds of fish, such as salmon and eels, divide their lifetime between fresh and salt water. Some, such as the goby, are smaller than your fingernail, while the whale shark (not a whale at all), the largest of all fishes, may be nearly fifty feet long. Some are flat like the butterfish and others long and snaky like the eel. Some have unusual fins with which they crawl along the sea bottom; then there are the flying fish that glide through the air. But all have bodies suited to swimming.

The streamlined bodies of most fish, their powerful muscles, and their fins equip them especially for life in the water. A fish has two pairs of fins and three single fins. The paired fins are to the fish what arms and legs are to us. The dorsal fin—the one on the back—is divided into two parts: one part sharp and spiny, the other soft. Then there are the anal fin and the tail fin. A fish swims by lashing the tail fin from side to side; the paired fins help it to turn and keep in balance; without them it would roll over and over. The dorsal fin helps in steering and stopping. The anal fin acts like the keel of a ship, stabilizing it.

Most fish have scales that overlap; the number of rows of scales and the color, that comes from the play of light on these, help to identify the different types. As the

Sunfish: (A) Paired fins; (B) Dorsal fin; (C) Anal fin; (D) Tail fin

fish grows, its scales add rings, and the age of the fish can be told from the number of rings. At the base of the scales are glands that secrete a slime which covers the scales, making the surface slippery so that swimming is easier. If you have ever tried to hold onto a fish by grasping its body you must have discovered just how slippery it is.

All animals need air, or oxygen, and fish get the oxygen that is dissolved in the water. For this they need gills. When a fish is cleaned you can see the red, soft gills which usually come paired in four layers, one set on each side of the head. A fish opens and closes its mouth with the same kind of rhythm used by other animals in breathing in and out. Two flaps on each side of the head cover the gills. These flaps also open and close. The water that comes into the mouth runs over the gills and out through the openings covered by the flaps. The gills have miles of tiny blood vessels with very thin walls. The dissolved oxygen is taken out of the water and absorbed into these blood vessels, and the carbon dioxide escapes through the

Left: Crappie; Right: Perch

same thin vessels. A strange kind of breathing this is—in water, and not in air!

Most fish have large mouths with teeth that curve inward. These rip and tear the food, and the curved ends prevent the food from escaping. The digestive tract is well developed and, in addition to the mouth, consists of a stomach, an intestine, and an anal opening. There is also a liver that helps to digest food. Nostrils, and taste buds in and around the mouth, are for smelling and tasting the dissolved chemicals in the water.

The fish has one eye on each side of the head. Fish eyes have no lids; water naturally keeps them free of foreign bodies. The ears in fish are inside the head. They are used mainly for keeping balance, and to let the fish know when it is right side up. On each side of the fish's body is a row of cells, like tiny pits or pores. This is the "lateral line" which enables the fish to feel currents and changing pressures. Thus, it is warned of the approach of other animals.

Some fish have air bladders inside the body. When these are filled with air, the fish rises to the surface. The air can be let out as if from a leaking balloon; then the fish can lower itself or else remain motionless in the water.

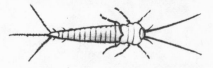

Here is a picture of a silverfish. You can see that it is not a fish; it doesn't resemble a fish

in any way. It is really an insect, a six-legged creature with antennae—more like a termite than a fish. It lives in damp places, often in houses, where it damages the bindings of books, wallpaper, and clothing.

And, of course, the sea horse is not a horse, but a fish that uses its tail as an arm for catching other fish as food.

FISH TYPES

There are four orders of fish, but the vast majority belong to the two modern orders: cartilaginous and bony. The other two orders—the gars and bowfin, and the lungfish are nearly extinct.

The Cartilaginous are more primitive, having a skeleton of cartilage and gill slits that are uncovered; they lack gill flaps. The shark, sting ray, and sawfish are examples of cartilaginous fish without true bones. Sharks have different scales, called placoids. These make their skin as rough as sandpaper. The shark has rows upon rows of

Tiger shark

teeth surrounding an enormously wide mouth. As the sharp edges of each row of teeth wear down, a new set of teeth replaces it, and the worn set drops to the bottom of the sea. Sharks' teeth have been covering the floor of the ocean for thousands of centuries.

A bony fish or *true* fish has a real backbone divided into segments; its head is made of bones, and its many other bones run parallel across both sides of the body. The minnow, rock bass, catfish, crappie, flounder, butterfish, salmon, herring, mackerel, perch, cod, haddock, marlin, menhaden, barracuda, sailfish, and flying fish are all bony fish. And you can probably name many others.

Fish have real hearts that pump blood through a

Mackerel

system of blood vessels. In the female an ovary produces eggs; in the male a sperm sac contains the sperm or milt. The mother fish lays eggs, a great many at a time, which she deposits in strings around water plants. The plants prevent them from floating away. When the father fish sprays the eggs with sperm, the eggs are fertilized and hatch into baby fish.

Lungfish have modified air bladders, perhaps the beginnings of lungs, which open into the throat. These come in handy when the water dries up; lungfish can survive a water shortage when other fish would perish. Fish are cold-blooded animals. That means that the body is as cold or as warm as the water in which they live. Warm-blooded animals like you and me get their warmth from inside their bodies. Cold-blooded animals require less oxygen than the warm-blooded, because their cells burn fuel more slowly.

All fish live in water, but not all animals that swim are fish.

Angel fish laying eggs around water plants

IN AND OUT OF WATER

We come next to animals that spend certain stages of their life in water and others on land.

They are called Amphibia. The name "amphibious," from the Greek, means "a double life." Salamanders and newts, frogs and toads are amphibians. They probably evolved from ancestors with primitive lungs. Their class name, Amphibia, refers to the way these animals develop. So let us trace the life-cycle of the familiar green frog.

The female frog lays its eggs in shallow water, and the male sprays its sperm over them. A sticky gelatin layer forms over the fertilized eggs and protects them as they develop into larvae. The larvae hatch into fishlike tadpoles. Tadpoles live in water, swim with a tail, and breathe with gills. Then hind legs form, and the tail and gills are slowly absorbed. Eventually front legs appear. The young frog is now ready to leave the water. As the gills disappear, the lungs begin to work and the tail is

Frog, tadpole, and eggs

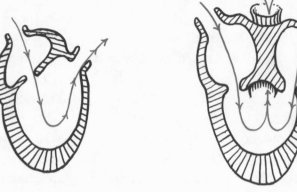

Tadpole heart   **Frog heart**

completely absorbed. The frog is now able to live on land.

Frogs have no scales, as you know, and their skin is always moist. This is a leftover from their ancestors' watery existence, and helps their breathing. A frog can "breathe" through its skin because oxygen can pass through thin cells in the moist skin.

While the frog can swim with its webbed feet. it also can hop on land with its powerful legs. If you have ever tried to catch one, you must have noticed how fast the frog can get away.

Another important change takes place during the metamorphosis of tadpole into frog. The tadpole, like a fish, has a two-chambered heart, and the land-inhabiting adult frog has a three-chambered heart, as you can see in the picture. The tadpole has an auricle which collects the blood from the body, and a ventricle which sends blood out through vessels to all parts of the body. The frog has two auricles and one ventricle.

The frog has still another structure that equips it for life on land. This is the sticky tongue at the front of its mouth which it flips out to catch insects. It also develops vocal sacs, with which the male frog croaks during mating time to serenade the female. Its eyes also have acquired lids—not two, but three. The third is transparent and is drawn over the eye when the head is under water. On land the frog's eyes protrude so that the animal can peep with great skill and spy a moving object. Unlike the fish, the frog has external ears behind the eyes so that warning signals are easily heard.

Salamanders develop in the same way as frogs, but the change from the water form to the adult land form takes less time. These amphibians are long-bodied like lizards, have weak legs, and keep their tails. They usually burrow in mud and moist cool places. They feed on snails, slugs, worms, and insects.

People sometimes confuse toads with frogs. Toads have a dry, warty skin, but the belief that they cause warts when handled is only a superstition. One toad, whose name is Surinam, has left the water entirely, and developed a different way of producing its young. It carries fluid-filled pouches on its back, where its young develop.

The Amphibia, in their double life, are a step away from the fishes and are the link with land-living vertebrates, the reptiles.

Green sea turtle

8

THE FIRST ON LAND

Fish, the first vertebrates, as we have seen, are completely dependent on a watery home. This is what is meant by "a fish out of water"—to describe being out of place. The Amphibia, it is said, "got three feet on land," but they still had to go back to the water to reproduce.

The reptiles were the first of the higher animals to become free of the bondage to water. They could live on land indefinitely. This tells us that they must be air-breathers with fully developed lungs. Of course, there are some that live in water, but they do not have gills even when they are very young. The huge sea turtle spends most of its life in water, but swims ashore to lay its eggs.

Nearly all reptiles have scales, and some have hard shells. Both scales and shells are exoskeletal structures. Are reptiles therefore like either fish or molluscs? You know the answer. Since they have a true bony skeleton and a backbone, they cannot be molluscs. Since they have no gills, they cannot be fish.

Then what makes a reptile a reptile? All reptiles have lungs and all are cold-blooded, regardless of differences among them. Snakes, turtles, alligators, crocodiles, and lizards are all reptiles. You would have no trouble distinguishing a turtle from a clam, or a crocodile from a fish. But many people confuse snakes with worms, legless salamanders, or eels—fish without paired fins.

You know that worms have no backbone. Salamanders have no scales, and their skin is moist and clammy. And as for eels—these have a soft dorsal fin and, of course, gills. So you see how you can tell the difference between reptiles and these other animals.

LEGLESS CRAWLERS

Snakes move with a wriggling motion that starts from the head and passes like a wave toward the tail. They hold fast to the ground by hard plates on the belly side. Legless, they manage to cover much ground swiftly by crawling, climbing, and swimming.

Snakes have many vertebrae and ribs—some have as many as 300—which explains why they can bend the body so easily. The ribs are not attached to a breast-bone, a strange arrangement that helps them in feeding, as you will see. Like the Arthropods, they molt, crawling out of their skin several times a year, and growing a new one. They have no eyelids; the eyes are protected by a transparent cap that is shed with the skin. Their ears are inside the body; in fact, a snake is deaf to sound carried by air. Its tongue is long, slender, and forked, used as an organ of touch and smell, not as a stinger.

The snake's feeding habits are often amazing. It darts out its tongue to feel. Needle-sharp teeth that curve inward are used as graspers rather than chewers. Its lower jaw bones are so loosely connected to each other and to the skull that the snake can separate them enough to swallow,

Pilot black snake

all in one piece, an animal two or three times the size of its head. Since the ribs are unattached, the body can stretch to accommodate the prey, which is gradually squeezed into the stomach. The powerful stomach juices go to work digesting the catch as soon as the lower end of the victim reaches the stomach.

Most snakes hatch from eggs laid on the sand, but some, including the common garter snake, bring forth their young alive, the eggs having hatched inside the mother's body. The young fend for themselves, and if necessary can go without food for months at a time.

People fear snakes because a few species are poisonous. Poisonous snakes—cobra, copperhead, rattler, and coral snake—have a pair of hollow fangs in the upper jaw, which connect with a poison sac. When the snake strikes, the fangs penetrate the flesh as a hypodermic needle does when the doctor gives you an injection, and the venom is forced into the wound. But even poisonous snakes try to avoid man and crawl to a hiding place.

The hognosed snake, sometimes called puff adder, is often thought to be poisonous, but is actually one of the most harmless kinds; the milk snake never steals milk from a cow.

It has been said that snakes are cannibals, eating their own kind. They do eat other snakes and lizards, as well as mammals. The king snake is very useful to the farmer because it kills mice and rats. It is immune to rattlesnake poison and actually hunts, catches, and eats these poisonous reptiles. Snakes can swallow another snake without stretching their bodies very much in any one place.

Copperhead snake

NO MATCH FOR THE HARE

Many people confuse turtles and tortoises. Turtles live in water; tortoises on land. The name "terrapin" is given those turtles whose flippers make good food. In Florida, and other places where they are caught, terrapin meat is a great delicacy on restaurant menus.

Even without the story of the tortoise and the hare, you know that turtles plod along very slowly indeed. This is because a turtle is enclosed in a hard shell, the upper part of which is cemented to its backbone, which greatly impedes movement.

The turtle has a short, broad body and four legs. In times of danger, the head, legs, and short tail are withdrawn into the shell for protection. If you can watch a turtle unobserved, you can see that its head and limbs are covered with the scales seen in all reptiles.

What chiefly sets turtles apart from other reptiles is their lack of teeth and their possession of a shelled armor. Instead of teeth they have horny ridges that serve the same purpose: they work like choppers. The shell has not only greatly modified the turtle's backbone but also its ribs, which do not meet in front, and are straight instead of curved. The turtle cannot expand its chest; as a result its method of taking in and expelling air has also changed. Air is drawn in by the contraction of two flank muscles and forced out by contraction of two pairs of belly muscles. This presses the internal organs against the lungs, pushing the air out. Some water turtles are able to use the throat lining as a sort of gill, to absorb a little oxygen when the animal is submerged in water for some time.

Turtles have still another way of taking in oxygen. Two sacs at the hind end alternately fill and empty themselves of water, through which oxygen is absorbed by way of the cavity that disposes of waste. Yet another way is the thorough ventilation of the lungs when there is plenty of air, alternated with the ability to "hold the breath" for as long as several hours. Because the turtle is cold-blooded, its modest need for oxygen is easily satisfied by these ways of breathing.

The turtle lays eggs with leathery shells, which it buries in the ground. But any hungry animal can and does dig them up because the mother turtle doesn't stay long with the nest. And immediately after hatching, the turtle is even more at the mercy of birds, mammals, and other reptiles. Because it has not yet built its shell, it makes a dainty morsel for any meat-eating marauder.

Turtles probably do not hear, or hear poorly, but they do have acute sight. When caught sunning themselves on a log, they will quickly escape into water if it is within

Pointed turtle, sunning on log

reach. The turtle's skin is also very sensitive to touch, the animal being able to feel the stroking of a straw along its skin, and even the scratching of its shell with the fingers.

The turtle is not fussy about its diet. It will eat any animals it can capture easily, and many kinds eat plants as well as animals, even if dead.

CROCODILE OR ALLIGATOR?

People often ask "Which is which?" At first glance they look very much alike. But except in a zoo, they are rarely seen together because of their geographical distribution. Crocodiles are tropical, and alligators—one species in China, the other in the southern United States—live in the temperate zone.

The crocodile has a long, narrow, and pointed snout; the alligator's snout is blunt, broad, and rounded. Another difference is that the crocodile's fourth tooth protrudes from the jaw. Alligators usually live in fresh water; crocodiles live in salty marshes and swim out to the sea.

Crocodile

The Crocodilians, as both are called, although they are in separate families, are the largest and heaviest of the reptiles. There are no small kinds among them. The large, heavy, and flattened tail is joined to the body, so that you cannot tell where the body ends and the tail begins. The powerful tail is a weapon of defense; with one sideswipe it can knock down a large enemy. The tail is used for swimming, while the legs, not nearly as powerful, carry the animal about on land. Contrary to hearsay, the crocodile does not drag itself; by means of its legs it raises its body off the ground and moves speedily. When frightened, it may slide down a slippery bank into the water.

The openings of the nose are on top of the snout, near its tip. When the animal is under water these openings allow air to get into the throat. At the same time it can keep its mouth open, ready to seize an animal. You and I cannot breathe and swallow at the same time. Try it. Some Crocodilians are ahead of other reptiles because they have a four-chambered heart like mammals, and

Alligator

their teeth are in separate sockets; they also have a primitive diaphragm, or at least a muscle in the middle of the body that is used in breathing.

Alligators and crocodiles are meat-eaters; the crocodile attacks big prey—large mammals, including man—but alligators are not as dangerous as people sometimes think.

FOUR-LEGGED AND SCALED

Lizards are sometimes confused with salamanders, but because of their scales they are easily set apart from the moist salamanders. Most lizards have four legs with five toes on each foot, although there are some species with elongated bodies and without a trace of a leg. Unlike snakes, lizards have movable eyelids. They recognize their prey by its movement, and they run easily and speedily. They have been clocked at fifteen miles an hour.

A few species with pads on their feet can climb on smooth surfaces, and some have structures that enable them to scale trees. They are harmless, except for the Gila monster in the southwestern United States which can inflict a painful bite. The horned toad is a lizard, not a toad, but has been called by that name because of the spines on its head.

The American chameleon is a special lizard that changes its color with its surroundings, and makes a popular pet. Many lizards are insect-eating creatures. When at rest, the tongues of these animals are kept folded in their mouths, but they can be shot out to the length of the body, to catch an insect on their sticky end.

American chameleon (lizard)

Spotted salamander

Horned toad (lizard)

9

EQUIPPED
FOR
FLIGHT

House sparrow

Compare the sparrow with the fossil reptile in the picture opposite. You would hardly believe them to be even distant relatives. Yet the record in the rocks shows that Archaeopteryx, that lived about 150 million years ago, was the first real reptile-bird. It was about the size of a crow, its jawbones were armed with teeth, and it had a long reptilian tail covered with feathers. Its tail bore little resemblance to the fan-shaped tails of birds. Yet the biologists say it was a beginning—a link to the modern feathered phylum *Aves*, the Latin name for birds.

Birds have no teeth. They are entirely covered with feathers; their light, hollow bones equip them for flight. Unlike reptiles they have a very rapid heartbeat; the heart is four-chambered; and they are warm-blooded, with a body temperature several degrees higher than man's. They maintain this temperature regardless of the temperature of the surroundings. What links them to their reptilian ancestors?

They still lay eggs, their feet are covered with scales, and their feathers have developed from the same skin cells as those of reptiles. There the resemblance ends.

Reptiles are generally sluggish; their metabolism, or rate of burning fuel, is low, they need little oxygen, and some can go without food when it is not available. Birds are "fast livers," have a high metabolism, seem to be eating all the time, and their powerful flight muscles generate a great deal of heat. There are other structures that help keep their bodies constantly warm.

Whether or not they fly, all birds have feathers. These prevent body heat from escaping. Beneath the outer feathers a layer of smaller (down) feathers traps air; like a blanket this helps to retain heat. Tiny skin muscles fluff the heavier feathers in cold weather, increasing the thickness of the insulation. Unlike the frog or snake, birds have a layer of fat under the skin that also helps to keep them warm.

Feathers have another function. Molting, usually once a year, enables birds to dress up in colorful feathers for courting and mating. Feathers are shed equally from both wings, so that flight is not disturbed.

The wing feathers, with long stiff quills, form a rigid

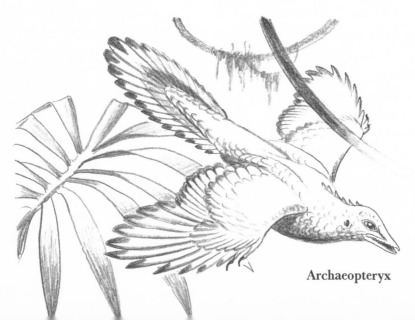

Archaeopteryx

surface to press against the air. The wing action lifts the light body, and as the wings "cut" the air, the pressure on top is lower than the pressure below them, keeping the bird in flight. The powerful flying muscles which, in fowl, form the "white meat," are attached to a keel-shaped breastbone; the tail, which acts as a rudder, and the streamlined body all adapt birds for flight.

EACH TO HIS OWN WAY OF LIFE

The family tree of birds has many branches. Some 20,000 different species are classified into twenty-seven orders. Their patterns of living—feeding habits, natural homes, way of moving, care of the young, nest-building, courting, and migration routes are fascinatingly varied. Some stride or walk, others swim or wade, and still others climb, run, or perch.

The feet of birds have a variety of uses, but chiefly they determine the type of movement. The many different shapes of beaks are also adapted to different jobs, but mainly to the special feeding habits of each type of bird. Legs, feet, and beaks are therefore important in birds.

Unlike most land animals with backbones, birds have three or four toes instead of five, the shapes of which differ according to whether they are waders, swimmers, runners, scratchers, or perchers. Let's take a look at some flightless birds.

GROUNDED BIRDS

The ostrich, the largest living bird, has long, powerful

legs capable of a twelve-foot stride, and it can match a horse in running. The Australian emu and the cassowary are also swift runners, and the tiny New Zealand kiwi, whose wings are practically nonexistent, is a walker on strong legs and long toes (birds walk on their toes rather than on their feet).

The penguin, also flightless, is webfooted, and its wings are modified into paddles, so that it is more at home in water than on land.

The sandpiper, that inhabits the Atlantic beaches, and its cousins, the plover and snipe, run along the seashore on long thin legs. Their wings are long, thin, and pointed, not very useful for high or sustained flight.

Left: Ostrich; Right: King penguin

The great blue heron, the stork, and the flamingo are wading birds with long legs; long slender toes help keep them balanced in mud and sand. Powerful wings carry large bodies from one muddy spot to another.

Loons and grebes, expert swimmers and divers, and ducks, geese, and swans, also water birds, have webbed toes for paddling through the water.

The quail, hen, and grouse have strong legs and feet adapted for scratching for food.

OTHER USES FOR FEET

The humming bird and the swift, whose extremely rapid wing motion carries them at great speeds, have weak legs.

The woodpecker is a champion climber; two of its toes point forward and two backward. So also the parrot,

Left: Canada goose;
Right: Downy woodpecker

Barn owl

which uses its feet for climbing, for holding food, and for clinging to objects. This arrangement helps it to climb the way you do when you use hands as well as feet on a steep incline.

Then there are the strong-clawed, grasping and tearing feet of the hawk, eagle, owl, and vulture—all birds of prey.

Many of the birds you see most often are perchers: wrens, starlings, blackbirds, crows, jays, robins, larks, swallows, finches, tanagers, and flycatchers. They all have three toes in front and one behind, fitted for grasping a twig. The toes are never webbed, and the hind toe is as long as the middle front toe. Even if the bird is asleep it maintains its perching posture. During sleep or rest, the knees and heels pull on the tendons; this causes the toes to curl and locks the bird automatically on its perch.

Bluejay

Downy woodpecker

Sparrow hawk

Bufflehead duck

Horned lark

Fox sparrow

STYLES IN BEAKS

Beaks are horny sheaths taking the place of jaws and teeth. The beak is used for food-getting, for preening, for oiling the feathers, and for nest-building. There are almost as many different sizes and shapes of beaks as of legs, permitting each type of bird to live under the special conditions of its surroundings.

The strong chisel-shaped beak of the woodpecker hacks away at the bark of trees as it digs for insects; hawks and vultures have strong curved and sharp beaks suited for tearing flesh; the flattened beaks of ducks and geese strain food from water and mud; larks and linnets have slender, delicate beaks for catching insects; herons and cranes have enormously long, sharp beaks with which to catch fish, frogs, and crustaceans, and to store them until they are ready to digest them; the seed-eaters, such as nuthatches, cardinals, finches, and sparrows, have strong bills which they use as nutcrackers to break the shells of seeds.

Not only feet and beaks, but wings also, are variously shaped. Soaring birds have broad wings; flapping birds pointed ones; and swift flyers are the ones with highly developed muscles attached to a keel-shaped breastbone. The albatross has wings

Wingspread of albatross

for gliding—long, slender and ribbon-shaped; swallows and terns that cruise all day in active flight have pointed, tapering wings for maneuvering.

GOOD PARENTS

Most fish, insects, and even reptiles lay their eggs and leave their young to grow up as best they can. But most birds take good care of their babies. Soon after mating, they are busy building nests. There they lay their eggs, warm them with their bodies, and one parent always keeps a close watch on the nest when the other leaves it to gather food.

When the young are hatched, some are covered with feathers, some only with down, and the young of songbirds, hawks, woodpeckers, and parrots are born naked. They stay in the nest until their feathers grow. The parents keep the young warm, feed them from mouth

Common tern

to mouth, and teach them to fly. Sometimes the mother bird stands off a few feet with a worm or a seed in its mouth tempting the young bird to try its wings. Gradually their muscles grow strong enough for them to fly away.

Some birds—chicks and running birds—are able to run and pick up food for themselves, but the mother hen still watches over them. She teaches them with warning calls and at night protects them under her wings. Baby geese have to be taught to swim. If they are taken from the mother too soon after hatching and put in a dish of water, they will drown.

What makes birds so protective of their babies? The full answer for this complicated behavior is not known. Scientists say it is because the parents, and especially the mother, produce hormones—chemicals from special glands—that provide the urge for caring for the young. Whatever the explanation, this habit of birds is an advance over the neglect of their young shown by lower forms of animals.

Which is *NOT* a bird?

Mallard duck

Ostrich

Chicken

White-throated
sparrow

Brown bat

Pileated woodpecker

Black-footed penguin

Little blue heron

Ruby-throated
hummingbird

ANSWER

A Bat. Do you know why? You will find the answer in
the next chapter.

10

WHAT'S NEW ABOUT MAMMALS?

Now that you know that a bat is not a bird and certainly not a member of any other lower phylum, you may guess that it must be a mammal. But here is how you can tell for sure. Its body is covered with fur; it has milk glands for feeding its young; and baby bats are completely formed inside the mother's body. That makes it a mammal, but it is the only flying mammal.

As a higher vertebrate the bat has some of the characteristics of a bird: it is warm-blooded, has a four-chambered heart, and well-developed lungs. But in addition, there are the fur and milk glands of a typical mammal.

If you put all these signs together you can recognize many animals you know as pets, or have seen in the zoo, in the field and woods, or on the farm. Cats, dogs, squirrels, rabbits, bears, lions, moose, monkeys, foxes, camels, elephants, chipmunks, cows, sheep, goats, horses, porcupines, raccoons, deer, weasels, woodchucks—the list seems endless, because there are about 12,000 different kinds of mammals.

You may not be so sure about the sea lion, beaver, seal, walrus, muskrat, and otter because these seem much more at home in water than on land. But don't let that fool you. Whales, dolphins, and the sea cow spend *all* their lives in water; in fact, they cannot move if they are stranded on land, but these also are mammals. Why? Because their babies develop inside the uterus, which is the organ inside the mother's body where they grow until ready to be born. The mother also nurses them after they are born. This is what makes them all mammals, getting their name from *mammae*, the milk-producing glands.

There is another new feature—the diaphragm, a dome-shaped muscle that divides the chest from the belly cavity. Only mammals have it and it is used in breathing.

Mammals, like other classes, have many differences as well as likenesses. For example, some are covered with fur and others with hair or wool on all or parts of the body; and some, like the whale, have almost none of either.

LEFT BEHIND IN THE MARCH

There are some four-footed animals that have left-over habits of the earliest mammals; in fact, they are the only survivors of a past age. In Australia we find the duck-billed platypus and the spiny anteater, fur-bearing animals that nurse their young, but lay eggs like turtles. Also in Australia—and you have seen it along with the platypus and anteater in the zoo—is the kangaroo. With the wombat and the opossum it belongs to the order of Marsupials. They give birth to underdeveloped young which remain in a pouch outside the mother's abdomen until fully developed.

**Left: Kangaroo;
Below: Armadillo**

The egg-laying mammals and the Marsupials form the first two orders of mammals. Then come the toothless or almost toothless sloth and armadillo. The sloth feeds on leaves, young shoots, and fruits. It lives in trees and hangs downward by hooklike claws. It is very awkward on the ground. The armadillo is covered by jointed bony plates that serve as protective armor. It runs with great speed, feeds on insects, worms, roots, and fruits, and, with its powerful claws, digs a hole in the ground to hide.

ARISTOTLE HAD A NAME FOR THEM

Nearly twenty-five centuries ago Aristotle distinguished the water-inhabiting mammals from the fishes. He gave them the name Cetaceans, which is still the name of the order of whales, porpoises (dolphins), and sea cows. He knew that their young were born alive and that they lived on mother's milk. This is what he wrote:

> "Among viviparous [born alive] animals are man, the horse, the seal, and other animals that are hair-coated and also, of marine animals, the Cetaceans. These latter creatures have a blow-hole and are provided with lungs and breathe. Thus the dolphin has been seen asleep with his nose above water, and snoring. The dolphin takes in water and discharges it through his blow-hole but he also inhales air into his lungs. . . ."

Aristotle knew that they take in water, because, he said, they get their food from the water. The blue whale—

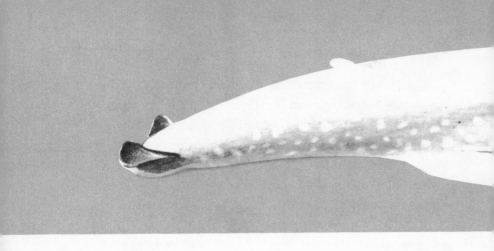

Blue whale

the largest beast that ever lived, weighing about as much as thirty elephants—feeds on plankton—masses of algae and millions of tiny animals. Practically hairless, it keeps warm in icy water with its thick coat of blubber. The whale swims with its tail and, with only two limbs—its

Beaver

flippers—it balances and steers its huge smooth and streamlined body.

THE GNAWERS

Far outnumbering human beings are the rodents, the largest order of mammals. Except for the beavers, rodents are usually small, inhabit every continent from the Arctic to the tropics, travel with man, breed frequently, and mature rapidly. Most of them do a great deal of damage. They have four cutting teeth, with sharp chisel-like edges, that keep growing throughout their entire lifetime. Some make good pets: white mice and hamsters. Some have valuable furs: muskrat, nutria, and beaver. But a great many (including the muskrat) are harmful: red squirrels, rats, meadow mice, gophers, prairie dogs (not dogs at all), porcupines, desert kangaroo rats, bog lemmings, and voles.

ODD-TOED AND EVEN-TOED

The hoofed animals are also a large order. They have

hoofs instead of claws, and broad, grinding teeth, suited to their vegetarian habits. Those with well-developed third and fourth toes are even-toed, and have divided hoofs. The sheep, antelope, ox, pig, camel, giraffe, deer, and the hippopotamus are among the even-toed. Many of these creatures are important to man. We use them as work animals, ride them, eat their flesh, drink their milk, and make leather from their hides.

The odd-toed have one well-developed toe, as in horses, zebras, deer, rhinoceroses, and tapirs; their hoofs are not divided.

INSECTS AND FLESH ON THE MENU

Next come the insect-eating mammals. They are small, plump animals, among them the shrew—the smallest mammal. The pigmy shrew weighs only a fifteenth of an ounce—less than a silver dime. The moles, shrews, and hedgehogs live in underground homes. To smell their way into tunnels, in search of worms and grubs, they have snout-like noses. They have muscular shoulders, shovel-like feet, and powerful claws that equip them for digging.

The bat belongs to another order of insect-eating mam-

Pigmy shrew, in its underground home

mals whose forelimbs form wings. A thin membrane is stretched over long fingers that support the wing-like structures. Closely related to the only flying mammal is the flying squirrel that moves with a gliding motion, and doesn't really fly. Bats are nearly blind, but have large ears that pick up the echo of their own extremely high-pitched sounds. This sound, which we cannot hear, echoes like a radar beam and guides the bat through the darkness of night, helping it to avoid obstacles and to locate flying insects for food.

The meat-eaters (Carnivores) are a group of familiar mammals, such as the cat and dog which have become domesticated, and the wild ones that hunt for their food. The lion, tiger, bear, raccoon, and weasel are wild, carnivorous beasts equipped with sharp claws and teeth for tearing their catch. The seal and walrus are water-inhabiting flesh-eaters.

PRIMATES—"FIRST IN RANK"

The word "primate" is from the Latin and means "first." This order, to which man belongs, was the last to develop, which means it is the highest in rank.

In this order many innovations have been introduced. It has nails instead of claws, and the big toe in the forelimb becomes a thumb in man. Most of these animals are four-footed, but the highest types use the forelimbs for grasping and the hind limbs for support. Primates have four canine, sharp-pointed tearing teeth, and eight incisors, or biting teeth. The eyes are set in deep sockets and are placed in the front of the head, instead of on each

Ring-tailed lemur   **Tarsier**

side. The eyes in Primates are therefore directed forward. With this arrangement they can see an object with both eyes, which helps to give the sense of depth.

You may have guessed from these details that Primates include the monkey, marmosets, and apes as well as man, but did you think of the lemur and tarsier, the lower members of this order? Except for the baboon and man, the Primates are all tree inhabitants, though the lower they are in the order, the more time they spend in trees. Their hands and feet are made for grasping and swinging on branches. Their nails protect the five fingers and toes of each limb. Those that have a tail use it as a balancing organ, and monkeys use the tail as a fifth limb for grasping.

Apes are nearly erect, supporting their weight on the

hind limbs, and using their forelimbs as we use our arms and hands. The anthropoid (man-like) apes are the orangutans, chimpanzees, gorillas, and the gibbons. The first three belong to the family of Pongidae, while the gibbon is sometimes considered as a separate family.

Closest to man are the chimpanzees and gorillas which make their home on the ground and rarely take to trees. The gorilla is a heavy-set, powerful animal, but despite its enormous size it has a brain less than half the size of man's. Chimpanzees are agile and can learn to do so many things that they are often featured in circuses and television shows. Some may be taught to skate, ride bicycles, use dishes and cutlery, and even to draw lines and to paint.

11

HERE *YOU* ARE

Man is one genus and species of the order of Primates: *Homo sapiens*—knowing, reasoning, and wise man—as explained earlier.

While mammals began to appear about sixty million years ago, it is estimated that man's existence on earth goes back only a million years. To be sure, the development of modern-day man went through several steps. These have been traced from parts of skeletons discovered in different parts of the world. Compared with other periods in evolution, the changes in man occurred rapidly. All the important changes were in the brain, hand, and thumb. These, as well as the use of language and the habit of living together in groups have made man the dominant form of all life.

Let's begin with the thumb. Touch each one of your four other fingers separately with the thumb, and then think of all the things you could *not* do if you could not use your thumb this way. Together with the development of the hand, and the long, freely jointed fingers, the thumb helped man use tools with great efficiency. He became a *doing* animal. With each more complicated movement of the hand, the brain grew in size, complexity, and flexibility.

Along with the growth of man's skill in handling tools, a thinking and reasoning brain developed. Also his speech organs changed so that he could use language to communicate with other men. At first he hunted animals for food; later, he gathered wild plants and seeds; still later, he learned to cultivate crops and to domesticate the dog, cattle, horses, and other animals.

Primitive man, hunting

Living in groups, man learned to obtain and store food, to build ever better shelter, to use ever more complicated tools, to build different means of transportation, to travel to places where life could be richer, and finally to teach his children to do all these things. This is what we mean when we say that man has learned to control his environment. Biologically man is related to his closest primate ancestors, but as a thinker, a doer, and a member of consciously organized society, he soars to ever greater heights and is, therefore, set apart from all other forms of life.

Since all men, regardless of their color or place of birth on the globe, have these qualities, there is only one species of man—one human race.

INDEX

Abalone, 80, 81

Agassiz, Louis, 35

Algae, 36; classification of, 34; kinds of, 37; as food, 37, 40, 116

Alligators, 92, 98–99; *see also* Crocodilians

Amebas, 11, 53, 54

Amphibia, 83, 89, 91, 92

Angiosperms, 45, 47, 48–51

Animalcules, 37, 117

Animals: with backbone, 14, 28; without backbone, 14, 26, 28, *see also* Vertebrates *and* Invertebrates; four-footed, 14, 113, 119; kingdom of, 29; differences and resemblances between plants and, 29–35; moving about of, 32; obtaining of energy by, 33–34; response of, to stimuli, 34; classes of, 34–35, 52; likenesses and differences among, 52; cold-blooded, 88, 92, 93, 97; warm-blooded, 88, 112; hoofed, 117–118; *see also* Birds, Insects, Mammals, *etc.*

Annelida, 61, 62, 65

Annuals, 42

Anteater, spiny, 113

Ants, 79–80

Apes, 120–121; anthropoid, 121

Arachnids, 73

Archaeopteryx, 102

Aristotle, 20, 28, 52; "ladder of nature of," 12–15; catfish named for, 35; quote from, on Cetaceans, 115

Armadillo, 115

Arthropods, 69–70, 72, 93

Aves, see Birds

Backbone, animals with and without, *see* Vertebrates *and* Invertebrates

Bacteria, 29, 34, 38; obtaining of food by, 32, 38–39; disease-producing, 38; uses of, 39

Barnacles, 32, 55, 70, 71

Bats, 111, 112, 118–119; description of, 112

Bees, 79

Beetles, 75–76, 77

Binomial system, 27

Bird, skeleton of, 15

Birds, 83, 102–110; grouping of, 14, 26, 35; beaks and claws of, 20, 104, 108; flesh-eating, 20, 107, 108; seed-eating, 20, 108; compared with reptiles, 102–103; feathers of, 102, 103–104; feet and legs of, 104–107, 108; flightless, 104–106; wings of, 105–106, 108–109; wading, 106; water, 106; of prey, 107; perchers, 107; as parents, 109–110

Bivalves, 66, 81

Blue whale, 115–117

Bryophytes, 36, 41, 43

Bugs, true, 77–78

Butterflies, 76–78

Carbon, formed by peat moss, 41

Carnivores, 119

Catfish, 35, 87

Cats, 27, 112, 119

Cells, 30–31, 41, 53–58, 85; description of, 30–31; male and female, 41; division of labor among, 55; coordination between, 56; double layer of, 56–57; epithelial, 57, 69; three layers of, 58; blood, in worms, 61

Centipedes, 70, 72

Cephalopods, 67, 81

Cetaceans, 14, 115

Chitin, 69, 75

Chlorophyll, 30, 32, 34, 37, 38, 41, 47

Chordates, 82

Ciliates, 54, 58

Circulatory systems, of animals, 34, 58, 61, 68, 71; of plants, 36

Clams, 32, 63, 65, 66, 68, 80, 81, 91

Classes, problems of arranging into, 12–17; of plants, 19–20, 36; of plants and animals, 24–25, 26, 34–35; of animals, 26, 53, 54; of Arthropods, 70; of insects, 75; of molluscs, 80–81; of vertebrates, 83

Clover, 26

Club mosses, 43

Coelenterates, 56–57, 61

Conifers, 46

Copepod, 72

Crabs, 55, 71

Crayfish, 70, 71

Crocodiles, 92, 98–99; *see also* Crocodilians
Crocodilians, 99–100
Crustaceans, 71–72
Cycads, 46

Daphnia, *see* Water flea
Darwin, Charles, 28
Diatoms, 37
Dicotyledons, 48–49
Digestive system, of animals, 56, 58, 60–61; of molluscs, 68; of crustaceans, 71
Dinosaurs, 42
Dogs, 27, 112, 119
Dolphins, 14, 115

Echinoderms, 62
Eels, 83, 93
Eggs, produced by plants, 41, 44; fertilization of, in plants, 47–48; development of, 60; of crustaceans, 72; of fish, 87–88, 109; of frogs, 89; of reptiles, 94, 97, 109; of birds, 102, 109; of insects, 109
Embryo, 49, 60
Energy, for plants and animals, 32–34
Equus, genus of, 26
Euglena, 29–30, 53–54
Evergreens, 46
Evolution, 27–28, 44, 53, 55, 61, 65; of man, 122–124
Exoskeletons, 69, 72, 92

Families, 26; of crocodiles and alligators, 99; of Primates, 121
Ferns, 17, 42–43
Fish, 83, 85–88, 92, 93; grouping of, 14, 26; fins of, 83, 93; scales of, 83–84, 86; gills of, 83, 84; eyes and ears of, 85; orders of, 86; cartilaginous, 86; bony, 86, 87; compared with reptiles and molluscs, 92; compared with mammals, 115
Flagellates, 29, 54, 55
Flatworms, *see* Planaria
Flies, 78
Flowers, reproductive parts of, 22, 47; plants without, 41, 42; plants with, 44, 47
Flukes, 58

Flytrap, 47
Food, how obtained by plants and animals, 31, 32–34, 37, 70; of fish, 37, 72; of clams, 68; of barnacles, 70; of snakes, 95; of turtles, 98; of Crocodilians, 100; of birds, 108; of sloths and armadillos, 115; of blue whale, 116
Fossils, 64, 74, 102
Frogs, 89–91, 103; life-cycle of, 89
Fruit, formation of, by plants, 47–48
Fungi, 36; plants classed as, 34; kinds of, 38; food for, 38–40; damage caused by, 39

Gars, 86
Gastropods, 66, 81
Genera (genus) 20, 25; of clover, 26; of cats and dogs, 27; of Primates, 122
Ghost crab, 72
Ginkgo, 46
Gnats, 78
Gnetales, 46
Goby, 83
Grasses, 17, 27, 35
Grasshoppers, 16, 75–77
Gymnosperms, 45–47

Hercules, 56
Hermit crab, 72
Homo sapiens, see Man
Horseshoe crab, 70, 74
Horsetails, 43
Hydra, 32, 56–57, 58

Insects, 70, 75–80; class of, 26, 34–35; straight-winged, 77; disease-carrying, 78; with sucking mouths, 80
Invertebrates, 14, 26, 27, 28, 65, 69, 75, 80–82

Kidney, beginnings of, in animals, 58
King crab, 74
Kingdoms, of plants and animals, 34–35, 52

"Ladder of nature," *see* Aristotle
Lamarck, Jean Baptiste de Monet, 28, 52
Larvae, of crustaceans, 72; of bees, 79; of frogs, 89

Leaves, shapes of, 17
Lemur, 120
Leopard, 27
Lichens, 40
Lilies, 17
Linnaeus, 18–27
Linné, Carl von, *see* Linnaeus
Lion, 27, 119
Liverworts, 41
Lizards, 92, 100; harmful, 100
L'Obel, Matthias de, 16, 49
Lobsters, 55, 70, 71
Locusts, description of, 16
Lungfish, 86, 88

Mammals, 83, 112–124; class of, 26; number of different kinds of, 112; water-inhabiting, 112–113, 115, 119; reproduction of, 113; differences and likenesses between, 113; egg-laying, 113, 115; orders of, 115, 117, 118–120; insect-eating, 118–119; meat-eating, 119; tree-inhabiting, 120–121; order of, 122
Man, 14, 119–124; skeleton of, 15; the reasoner, 27; first appearance of, 122; development of, 122–124
Marsupials, 113, 115
Metamorphosis, of insects, 76–79; of frogs, 89–90
Mildews, 38, 39
Millipedes, 70, 72
Mistletoe, 47
Mites, 73
Molds, 32, 34, 38–39
Molluscs, 65–68, 80–81; compared with fish and reptiles, 92
Molting, of Arthropods, 69; of snakes, 93; of birds, 103
Monocotyledons, 48–49
Mosquitoes, 78
Mosses, 41, 42; true, 43
Moths, 78
Moufet, Thomas, 16
Mushrooms, 32, 34, 38, 39; *see also* Toadstools
Mussels, 66

Naturalists, early, 12, 14–17, 18, 28
Nautiluses, 68
Nervous system, of animals, 58, 61–62, 71
Notochord, 82

Octopuses, 65, 67–68, 80, 81
Opossum, 113
Orchids, 17, 47
Orders, 25, 26; of Gymnosperms, 46; of insects, 75–80; of fish, 86; of mammals, 114, 117–124; of Cetaceans, 115
Ovary, 47–48
Oysters, 63, 65, 66, 68, 80, 81

Paramecium, 53, 54
Parasilurus aristotelis, 35
Parasites, 38; among Angiosperms, 47; among worms, 58–60, 62
Peat moss, 41
Penicillin, from bread mold, 39
Perennials, 42
Phleum, *see* Timothy
Photosynthesis, process of, 32; of horsetails, 43
Phyla (phylum) of plants, 36, 41; of animals, 52, 53, 55; of worms, 58, 60, 61; of invertebrates, 65–66; of Arthropods, 70, 72; of Chordates, 82; of birds, 102
Pistil, 47
Planaria, 53, 54–55, 58, 61
Plankton, 37, 70, 116
Plants, classes of, 19–20, 34, 35, 36; kingdom of, 29; differences between animals and, 29–35; motion of parts of, 31–32; obtaining of energy by, 32–34; response of, to stimuli, 34; organs and systems of, 34; seed-bearing, 42, 44–51
Platypus, duck-billed, 113
Pollen tube, 44, 47
Pongidae, 121
Porifera, *see* Sponges
Porpoises, 115
Primates, 119–124
Protoplasm, 29–31, 54
Protozoa, 29, 55, 61; species of, 53
Pseudopods, 53
Pteridophytes, 36, 41–43

Reproduction, ways of, 14, 44, 46, 47; of animals, 31; of plants, 31, 41, 44–45, 46, 47; organs of, in worms, 58; of Arthropods, 70; of insects, 76–77; of mammals, 113
Reptiles, 26, 42, 83, 96, 100, 102; scales and shells of, 92; compared

with fish and molluscs, 92; compared with birds, 102–103
Resin, 46–47
Rodents, 52, 117
Roots, plants with and without, 41–44
Roundworms, 58, 60–61
Rusts, 38

Salamanders, 91, 93, 100
Sand-dollars, 63–64
Sarcodina, 53
Scales, of fish, 83–84, 86; of reptiles, 92; of turtles, 96; of lizards, 100
Scallops, 66, 80, 81
Scorpions, 70, 73
Sea cows, 115
Sea-cucumbers, 64
Sea horse, 86
Sea-lilies, 64
Sea turtle, 92
Sea-urchin, 63
Seaweed, 37
Segmented worms, 58, 61, 65; blood-sucking, 62
Shark, 86–87
Shells, of molluscs, 66–67, 68; of reptiles, 92
Shrimp, 70, 71
Silverfish, 86
Snail, 65, 66, 80, 81
Snakes, 92–95, 103; poisonous, 94–95; superstitions about, 95
Sowbug, 53, 55, 71, 72
Sparrow, 102, 108
Spartina townsendii, 35
Species, 25, 26, 27; changing of, 28; discovery of new, 35; of Thallophytes, 36; of Angiosperms, 47; of protozoa, 53; of Arthropods, 70; of birds, 104; of Primates, 122; of man, 124
Sperms, produced by plants, 41, 44; of fish, 87–88; of frogs, 89
Spermatophytes, 36, 43–44
Spiders, 70, 73
Sponges, 55, 61
Spores, 41; growth of ferns by, 42
Squid, 65–68, 80, 81
Squirrels, 117, 119

Stamen, 47
Starfish, 63
Stentor, 53, 54
Stimuli, 34, 53
Structure, grouping by, 27–28, 34
Surinam, 91
Symbiosis, 40
Systema Naturae, 24

Tadpoles, 89, 90
Tapeworms, 58–59
Tarsier, 120
Termites, 79
Terrapin, 96
Thallophytes, 36, 40
Ticks, 70, 73
Tiger, 27, 119
Toads, 91
Toadstools, 38, 39
Tortoises, 96
Tournefort, Joseph Pitton de, 19–20
Townsend, Frederick, 35
Trifolium, *see* Clover
True bug, 77–78
True worms, *see* Segmented worms
Trypanosomes, 29
Turtles, 92, 96–98
Two-name system, *see* Binomial System
Typhoid bacillus, 29

Vacuoles, 31
Vermes, class of, 26
Vertebrates, 14, 26, 28, 82, 83, 92, 93, 112
Vinca minor, 31
Vorticella, 29, 30

Wastes, systems for discharging, 61, 71
Waterbugs, 70, 78
Water-flea, 53, 55, 71, 72
Whale shark, 83
Whales, 14, 115; blue, 37, 115–117
Wings, of birds, 105–106, 108–109
Wolf, 27
Worms, parasitic and non-parasitic, 58, 62; phyla of, 58, 60, destructive, 59–60; blood-sucking, 62; *see also* Flatworms, Roundworms, *and* Segmented worms

Yeasts, 32, 34, 38, 39

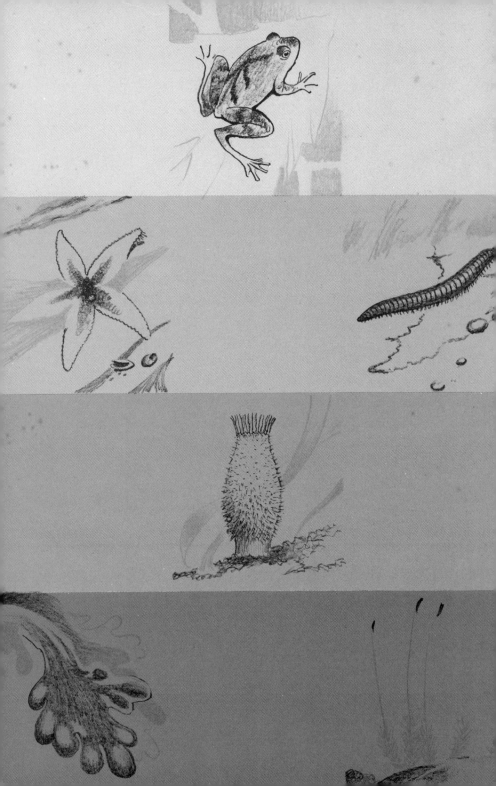